That Lawyer Girl

The Unauthorized Guide to Ally's World

A. C. BECK

BOOKS

RENAISSANCE BOOKS
Los Angeles

Thanks to:

Brenda Scott Royce, Renaissance Books;

Jonathan Rosenthal, Museum of Television & Radio;

Sue Schneider, Flower Children, Ltd.;

Raechel Fittante, research assistance;

Biff L. "Fist" Peterson, spiritual guidance;

and Peter Rubie, Perkins, Rubie & Associates.

Library of Congress Cataloging in Publication Data
Beck, A. C.
    That lawyer girl : the unauthorized guide to Ally's world / A.C. Beck.
        p. cm.
    Includes index.
    ISBN 1-58063-044-8 (pbk. : alk. paper)
    1. Ally McBeal (Television program) I. Title.
PN1992.77.A533B43   1999
791.45'72—dc21   98-55396
                                                           CIP

10 9 8 7 6 5 4 3 2 1
Design by Hespenhide Design

Manufactured in the United States
Distributed by St. Martin's Press
First Edition

Contents

Part I: The Show

Part II: The Cast

Part III: Episode Case Reviews

Part One
The Show

Chapter 1
Getting a Grip

Ally McBeal is a TV show.

Not a documentary. Not a declaration of the Way Things Should Be. Not an instruction manual on How People Should Live. Not a Guide to Friggin' Life.

It's a TV show.

Specifically, it's a lawyer show—like a hundred *Perry Mason*s to come before it.

Granted, its title character paces the courtroom in illicit heels, compares the law to yeast infections and talks penis size in a unisex bathroom.

And granted, stone-faced Perry Mason would never go there—particularly to the unisex.

But big deal—these are immaterial style concerns. Perry Mason's a fake TV lawyer; Ally McBeal's a fake TV lawyer.

The bottom line: *Ally McBeal* is a TV show.

Just so we get things straight from the start.

(P.S.: The woman who plays Ally McBeal? Calista Flockhart? She's an actress. Not an advocate for the revocation of the Nineteenth Amendment. Not a pusher of size 2 clothes. . . . But we get ahead of ourselves.)

Creator David E. Kelley's comedy/drama series about a young, Boston-based litigator—a sort of twisted, sideways Mary Richards—premiered on Fox on September 8, 1997. Its *Perry Mason* roots aside, *Ally* played like *L.A. Law* meets *thirtysomething* on a *Sisters*-recommended estrogen regimen.

Kelley's gift was to make the mix seem new and important. Not since ABC–TV's *thirtysomething* (1987–91)—the Emmy-winning examination of the tribal rites of self-reflective baby boomers—had a show inspired a greater "love it or hate it" vibe.

If his heroine wasn't being slammed for defacing the memory of Susan B. Anthony, she was being touted as the product of quality television. If she wasn't being criticized for belittling the work of lawyers, she was being applauded by fans who found their insecurities, their petty faults, mirrored in her own.

Ally was at the center of a minor cultural tug-of-war— but why? Slow week in Washington? Slow decade in the millennium? Nothing else good on?

There was a little something to each of those three possible motives. But also consider Kelley's mission for his title character in the series' very first episode:

1. Pop up on screen in a Heather Locklear–regulation microskirt;
2. Fantasize a steamy clinch with a guy in a giant coffee cup;
3. Pretend breasts are really, really big.

Kelley's Ally didn't burn a bra. She didn't bar a friend from going to a NOW rally. She didn't deliver a Phyllis

Schlafley stump speech. She didn't walk around with a sign, declaring, "Look at me—I'm the new representation of the postfeminist ideal! . . . Please, feel free to whistle."

Ally simply told its story in the language of good old-fashioned TV sex. *That* was the grabber. Americans love nothing, if not talking and watching and arguing TV sex. It's so much . . . *tidier* than real sex.

TV sex is clever talk, kisses, double-entendres, and maybe, if you're watching *NYPD Blue*, a lovingly lit bare butt. It provides tailor-made fodder for morning TV news shows, afternoon TV talk shows and *Glamour* magazine polls: Does size really matter? What are the ramifications of a one-night stand? . . . Blah, blah, blah, blah.

Nice. Neat. Provisionally provocative—enough to make the audience member think, "I'm so glad I'm hip to this and not a close-minded twit like my ancestors."

Real sex, on the other hand, is unsettling—from Howard Stern's radio and TV freak shows, to the relatively mild unadulterated text of the Bill Clinton–Monica Lewinsky papers. Real sex keeps news directors on restricted diets of Tums tablets as they agonize whether Americans are ready to hear "oral" in front of the word "sex."

True, *Ally* winked at oral sex—a visual gag with cappuccino foam being one of its supremely sly tubeland moments. But that's what TV sex does best—*it winks*. And, in the 1997–98 TV year, nobody winked better than *Ally*.

The show titillated. The show intrigued. And because it doesn't take much to send viewers (and even critics) over the edge, it unsettled.

Consider:

- *Ally McBeal* is "everything [you] want in a series . . . smart, fresh, funny, warm, wry and well-produced" (*TV Guide*). Or it's a "simpering drag" (*Time*).
- *Ally McBeal* is "maddeningly erratic" (*Newsday*). But "worth watching every week anyway" (same newspaper, same review).

What was that all about? That was about *Ally* unsettling. Getting under skin. In a TV-sex kind of way.

Okay, the *Time* magazine cover—how to explain that? How to explain *Ally* landing on the cover of *Time* freakin' magazine? If it's *just* a TV show, what's it doing up there?

Didn't the cover of *Time* used to mean something? Like you were a world-class god (Albert Einstein) or demon (Adolf Hitler)?

Supposedly. But there was *Ally* anyway: front and right of center, on the June 29, 1998, issue. Looked like Serious Stuff, too: a black-as-night background, a grim, taking-stock headline ("Is Feminism Dead?") and four mug shots, lined up like tombstones—Susan B. Anthony, Betty Friedan, Gloria Steinem, Ally McBeal.

Since when did a primetime TV series—much less a make-believe person—rate joining the company of a U.S. mint–approved suffragette (Anthony) and two future postage stamps (Friedan and Steinem)?

"Susan B. Anthony would roll over in her grave," Flockhart said in *TV Guide*.

Exactly.

Sort of.

CALISTA FLOCKHART PLAYS TV LAWYER ALLY MCBEAL—A MAKE-BELIEVE
PERSON NOT TO BE CONFUSED WITH SUSAN B. ANTHONY'S WORST
NIGHTMARE.
© JEAN CUMMINGS/FLOWER CHILDREN LTD.

Maybe only an activist like Anthony, an individual who fought for the magnanimous causes of one woman, one vote, and equal pay for equal work, could appreciate that *Time* is entitled to its opinion—however stupid it may be.

Since we've already established that *Ally McBeal* is just a TV show, let the record further state: *Ally McBeal cannot* be the endgame of feminism. *Cannot* be Susan B. Anthony's worst nightmare. And, presumably, *is not* keeping Betty Friedan or Gloria Steinem up nights with nagging, awful worry.

Pretty simple stuff. Couldn't the powers-that-be at *Time* figure that out? Or did they honestly believe Kelley was on a

Reel—er, Real Boston

Ally McBeal is no *Spenser: For Hire* (1985–88). That Robert Urich P.I. drama was a Boston-based show filmed in Boston. Outside of a few picture-post-card skyline shots, *Ally* is a Boston-based show filmed in Los Angeles—well, Hollywood (Season No. 1) and Manhattan Beach (Season No. 2). In 1997, star Calista Flockhart told the *Boston Globe* that she, in fact, hadn't set foot in the Massachusetts metropolis (1990 census population, approximate: 575,000) since she was a child. Still, "I think the show has a Boston feel," she said, adding with a bit of *Ally*-esque logic: "It feels very East Coast, even though it's hard to imagine sometimes because it is L.A."

Uh-huh.

Well, should you be so inspired to imagine Boston in person, as part of a quasi-*Ally* pilgrimage, here are some key tourist stops:

Suffolk County Superior Court: Referenced early and often on *Ally*, this house of would-be justice is located at 55 Pemberton Square. Watch real-life attorneys argue real-life cases. (Sorry, they're probably not going to be nearly as cute as the TV ones.) Afterward, toast our legal system at one of the dozen-plus bars and pubs located no more than a mile from the courthouse. A few of the more intriguing-sounding venues: **The Littlest Bar** (47 Province Street), **Sneaky Pete's** (26 Lagrange Street) and **Charlie Flynn's** (228 Tremont Street). (Sorry, they're probably not going to feature Vonda Shepard at the piano.)

Boston Bar Association: Another prime location (16 Beacon Street) to spot real-life Beantown lawyers. (Not that you'd want to call them "*Beantown* lawyers" to their faces. Locals often bristle at tired, clichéd nicknames. Try something more inventive, like, "clam-chowder heads," perhaps.) Once

you're done perusing legal eagles (or running for your life after trying out the "clam-chowder heads" line), scoot on over to **Neiman Marcus** (5 Copley Place), a mere mile away, for a brand-new washcloth—er, skirt.

Fenway Park: A no-brainer of a stop. *Ally* fan or no, if you're in Boston, you *must* see the legendary baseball home/palace of the Boston Red Sox (4 Yawkey Way). The best reason? The best reason to see any old ballpark: Catch it before somebody tears it down and erects a parking lot/shopping mall/sports complex/luxury box paradise in its place. The stadium has stood since the 1912 season. Ted Williams, Carl Yastremski and—as of Season No. 2 episode "The Real World"—Ally McBeal, have all roamed its grounds. Ms. McBeal was the first to do it in virtual form. According to an Internet newsgroup post by series visual F/X supervisor Michael Most, the baseball scenes involving the actors (Flockhart and guest star Richard Lee Jackson) were filmed three thousand miles away on a field at California State University, Fullerton. Their actions were later married to specially shot Fenway footage. That said, the best special effect at Fenway is a very real one—left field's Green Monster.

New England Aquarium: Occasionally referenced as a dateworthy destination on *Ally*, the Aquarium is the place to go sea life–exploring, whale-watching and, as of 2000, IMAX movie–watching. For more information, check out its Web site at http://www.neaq.org.

Harvard University: All right, so this isn't *really* in Boston. But it *is* a mere commuter hop to Cambridge (24 Quincy Street, to be precise—not that you need the address for this one; locals probably will have a pretty good idea where to direct you). In any case, consider this a must-see. Harvard is a key setting for *Ally* (the show's namesake heroine is an alum), not to mention Erich Segal's weepy-supreme novel (and movie), *Love Story*. Plus, Harvard is also supposed to be this place where future captains of industry and government get real smart, so that might be kinda cool to check out, too.

nefarious mission to ridicule and undermine the modern
working woman?

Here's two theories:

1. In the summer of 1998, nothing guaranteed an attention-
grabbing cover like *Ally McBeal*. Its mastery of the TV-sex
game was, in a word, masterful. There were virtually no media
conversations about male-female relations (and, thanks to the
unisex, bathroom habits) without a nod to *Ally*. It was
debated as often on the op-ed pages as it was on the entertainment pages.

If *Time* was going to make its dubious "death of feminism" point, it might as well make it with *Ally*.

What *Time* knew, what every pop-culture junkie worth
his *Entertainment Weekly* subscription knew, was that *Ally
McBeal* was the "It" show of 1998.

Modern-day attention spans being what they are (i.e.,
largely dependent on the availability of a Ritalin prescrip-
tion), *Ally*'s reign as the "It" show of the 1997–98 TV year
was sandwiched somewhere between *Buffy the Vampire
Slayer* and *Dawson's Creek*—aka, the season's other "It"
shows.

But in its glory months? It *was* glorious. The news-
stands were full of *Ally* and its stars. They were everywhere
that "It" shows and stars want to be: on the covers of *Cosmo,
TV Guide, Self, Time* (natch)—and, yes—*Entertainment
Weekly*.

(Come to think of it, making the cover of *EW* in the
1990s was the pop-culture milestone that making the cover of
Time, or its sister *Life*, was in the 1940s—thus rendering

Time's latter-day Susan B. Anthony–vs.–Ally send-up not only silly, but irrelevant.)

But, no matter, thanks to *Ally*'s drawing power, the show didn't render *Time*'s issue impotent. It got talked about. It got bought.

And wasn't *that* the point?

Well, one of them, maybe.

The second theory:

2. *Time* ran with the *Ally* cover because its collective editorial staff lost it—lost its grip. Started confusing TV people for real people. Started confusing individual characters for symbolic characters.

Time was far from alone. The *New York Times*, *GQ* and *Newsweek*—among dozens of others—all ran think pieces on *Melrose Place*'s Monday night time-slot companion.

It's not wrong to wax important on TV. This whole book is a would-be think piece on TV. The difference is, this book is *not* a think piece on why *Ally McBeal* is a bad/good influence on the Spice Girls generation. Or why Calista Flockhart is setting an unhealthy image ideal for third-graders in Iowa.

It's about why we bother to think such things in the first place.

"Really, the conclusions I've come to is that I don't care whether they like *Ally McBeal* or whether they hate *Ally McBeal*," Flockhart said in *Cosmopolitan*.

"To me the really interesting question is why people care so much. . . ."

Bingo.

It's hard to imagine a scenario where *Ally McBeal* is still debated or discussed ten years down the road in terms other than: "That was a funny show sometimes, huh?"

Nothing—except maybe *Ally*'s ability to provoke witless arguments as to whether the lead character would make a good lawyer in "real life"—lasts forever. "It" shows become "hit" shows become "well, there's nothing else on" shows.

Wham. Bam. When's *Felicity* on?

The only pop-culture artifacts to consistently inspire debate on a decade-after-decade basis are Bergman films and rock albums from the 1960s—a *Sgt. Pepper's Lonely Hearts Club Band*, say—and that's only because everybody was too stoned to hear and see the things right the first time.

Fortunately, for most of us, *Ally* is crystal-clear—and of the moment. When the moment passes, we'll move on to something else. This is not to diminish or discount what *Ally* is or will be, it's just a reminder: This, too, shall pass.

In ten years' time, it might be difficult to remember why *Ally* was *Ally*. Why the show made people lose their senses. Start arguments. Tune in every week.

Hopefully, this book will offer some clues.

It'll examine the show's history (such as it is), its players, its episodes. It'll throw out theories: the TV sex thing, the *Three's Company* angle, the Vonda Shepard factor. It'll be subjective and critical and arguably full of it.

And, ultimately, it'll be a book about a TV show.

Nothing more, nothing less.

Chapter 2
The Dress

The 1997–98 Primetime Emmy Awards. September 13, 1998. Los Angeles' Shrine Auditorium.

Ally McBeal, the break-out hit of the past season, is nominated in ten categories, the best showing, by far, of any new series. It is slotted in the comedy competition—a seriously farcical hourlong show up against the yuk-yuk sitcom likes of *3rd Rock from the Sun*. Its star, Calista Flockhart, is on hand to defend her Golden Globe win, where earlier she had been named best actress in a comedy. Can she beat Oscar-winner Helen Hunt (*Mad About You*)? Could she possibly lose to someone (Kirstie Alley) from . . . (gasp!) *Veronica's Closet*?

Also of note: *Ally* creator David E. Kelley. Arriving with movie-star wife Michelle Pfeiffer on his arm, the one-man TV industry stands to dominate the night. Not only is *Ally* nominated for best comedy, his *other* lawyer series, ABC-TV's *The Practice*, is nominated for best drama.

Okay, that's the rundown. Those are the *Ally*-related story lines for Emmy night. As TV news goes, they're not half-bad.

And before the night's even over, they don't mean diddly. Because of Calista Flockhart's dress.

CALISTA FLOCKHART AT THE 1997–98 PRIMETIME EMMY AWARDS IN 'THE DRESS'—THE CHERNOBYL OF FASHION DISASTERS.

© PAUL FENTON/FLOWER CHILDREN LTD.

The aforementioned Ms. Flockhart walks the media-surrounded red carpet in a pale pink Richard Tyler thing—no sleeves, no back.

Lots of trouble.

She looks too bony, too frail, too Audrey Hepburn, in a terminal-cancer sort of way.

That's what the wags are wagging, anyway.

Fast-forward a couple months and nobody really remembers who won at the Emmys. Nobody really remembers that Helen Hunt took the best lead comedy actress statuette. Nobody really remembers that Calista Flockhart lost or that *Ally* got all but shut out. What everybody remembers is that Calista Flockhart wore a pale pink Richard Tyler "sheath" that supposedly made her look too bony, too frail, too Audrey Hepburn, in a terminal-cancer sort of way.

Why?

Because *Ally* is *Ally* is *Ally*. What's going on outside of the show is seemingly predestined to be more important than what's going on inside.

The road to Emmy night was pretty much like Emmy night itself—a circus all the way. In the fall of 1997, Fox launched *Ally* with all the hype befitting the only new show on its schedule it figured people would actually watch. (*Cops 2*, anyone?) Even before its premiere, it declared that the show was "sure to become one of [the season's] most talked about new series."

The circus was coming to town.

On September 8, 1997—in the time slot following *Melrose Place*—viewers finally got to check out the thing for themselves. What they saw was this: Somebody named

Calista Flockhart as title character Ally McBeal, a young lawyer prone to voice-over thoughts, special-effect fantasies and general lust for her ex-boyfriend; somebody named Gil Bellows as Ally's ex-boyfriend Billy Thomas—as of the pilot, a coworker at the law firm of Cage/Fish Associates; somebody named Greg Germann as the cold Fish of Cage/Fish; somebody named Lisa Nicole Carson as Renee Radick, Ally's reality-grounded roommate and sometime-courtroom adversary (she's a prosecutor); and somebody named Jane Krakowski as Elaine Vassal, the tarty, nosy, annoying Cage/Fish secretary. And for *Melrose Place* fans, there was Alison—er, Courtney Thorne-Smith as Georgia Thomas, Billy's Barbie-doll wife with the Barbie-doll hair.

Okay, maybe a few of these faces were familiar. *Ned and Stacey* registered in the Nielsens during its brief run, right? The name and/or face of costar Greg Germann perhaps rang a bell? And Peter MacNicol, the actor who would join the regular cast six episodes into the season as the eccentric Cage of Cage/Fish—he looked like somebody, didn't he? No matter. *Ally* had all the stars it needed at premiere time: writer-producer David Kelley. The Steven Bochco (*Hill Street Blues*, *L.A. Law*) disciple had a rep for well-received, if not block-buster, TV. *Picket Fences*, *Chicago Hope*, *The Practice*—they were all his, too. They all made the vast wasteland a little less vast. They all ensured that *Ally* would get a serious look by critics. Aaron Spelling (*Charlie's Angels*, *Beverly Hills 90210*, *MP*...) or Darren Star (*MP*)—these producer guys come up with the same series? They pitch a show wherein the lead lawyer struts around in a glorified loincloth? No chance.

Critics dismiss it as so much T&A ratings pandering. But Kelley does it? Hey, it's pushing-the-envelope TV.

Is that the circus up ahead?

This is the way Emmy night was supposed to go:

First, it was supposed to be the capper. An evening to bask in The Year of *Ally*—all the good reviews (the *San Francisco Chronicle*'s ". . . the first great show of the season" being as good a blurb as any); all the ratings-driving controversies (see: *Time* magazine); all the style-setting gimmicks (the unisex, the skirts, the pajamas, the Dancing Baby . . .); all the awards (the Golden Globes, the Viewers for Quality Television honors . . .).

Second, it was to officially christen Flockhart as the Next Big Star. Granted, by September 1998, she was already pretty big. (*Ally*, as it turned out, being the sort of show that didn't need names—it *made* them.) But winning a Golden Globe is one thing, winning an Emmy is another. Pia Zadora—she's got a Golden Globe. But you have to be at least Craig T. Nelson (*Coach*) to win an Emmy.

Third, it was to officially declare *Ally* the best—and let its social critics be damned.

That's the way things were *supposed* to be. Then there's the way things were.

Which brings us back to The Dress.

Frasier won Outstanding Comedy Series. Hunt won Outstanding Lead Actress in a Comedy Series. *Ally* won Outstanding Sound Mixing—an honor dispensed during the

nontelevised portion of the techie awards, no less. On black-tie Emmy night, the only *Ally* player to take the stage in victory was David Kelley—and that was to accept an Outstanding Drama Series win for *The Practice*.

Ally's dream night, it appeared, had fizzled.

Only not really.

Ally didn't need awards. Heck, it could be argued the thing didn't need ratings. Where did the series finish the 1997–98 Nielsen race? Top ten? Top twenty? Try number 57—a tenth of a point behind stuff like *George & Leo*. What was *George & Leo*? Dead meat. What was *Ally*? The "most talked-about new series."

Ally was its own phenomenon. Its success, its importance, its influence, all magnified to epic proportions.

If Flockhart had appeared at the Emmys in a cover-up potato sack and *Ally* had swept the awards, the night wouldn't have meant as much to the overall *Ally* lore as the show winning nothing and Flockhart being branded an anorexic and a poor role model for young girls.

The way things were *supposed* to be? The Dress imbroglio was *exactly* the way things were supposed to be.

As always, *Ally* was its own phenomenon.

And this is the story of how it got there.

Chapter 3
Melrose Place Needs
a Neighbor

Anyone who thinks David E. Kelley (perhaps in a cabal with that skinny Flockhart person) set out with *Ally* to craft a bold statement on feminism doesn't know the biggest cliché about network TV: It's all about the ratings. "Bold" rarely helps sell diapers and minivans and toilet paper—and other fine products of stalwart network sponsors. "Bold" rarely posts big numbers; it's much easier for audiences to watch a conveniently laugh track–equipped *Home Improvement* than a slightly visually demanding *Police Squad*. "Bold" rarely entices: it takes Norman Lear three pilots to get *All in the Family* on the air; it likely takes all of three seconds to greenlight a new vehicle for the Olsen twins.

The bottom line on "bold": Unless it involves a guy stringing a strand of spaghetti through his nose, networks hate it.

So don't think Fox executives went head-hunting for a bold, important new series designed to turn back the clock on the women's movement. They went head-hunting for a hit.

In many ways, *Ally*—with its talent for potty jokes, TV sex and scantily clad women—was no different from the hits

Fox usually searched out. The Rupert Murdoch network began its primetime life in April 1987 with a simple mission: ratings, by any means necessary. It was not a new mission. *The Beverly Hillbillies* wasn't exactly programmed by the CBS of the 1960s to bring to light the plight of displaced Appalachian residents in a wealthy Los Angeles enclave. It was programmed because it aimed just low enough to deliver a mass audience. When Fox took on the Big Three (ABC, CBS, NBC) in the late 1980s, it was in something of a fix. If lowest-common-denominator programming was what sizzled, how could an upstart possibly hope to top, so to speak, *Perfect Strangers* or *Who's the Boss*. On one hand, the Big Three had the market cornered on no-account ratings grabbers. On the other hand, as Murdoch's bold-faced, headline-screaming newspaper empire proved, his camp was more than up to the challenge.

The first on-air hire by Fox was Joan Rivers, a solid stand-up who wrote her ticket to star status on the basis of Elizabeth Taylor fat jokes. Her *Late Show* contract was a sign of low-rent things to come. When Fox launched its abbreviated primetime schedule, its crown jewel was *Married . . . With Children*, a sitcom ostensibly designed as the anti–*Cosby Show* and effectively tooled to work shock-laughs from the sure-fire topics of boobs, smelly shoes and sexual dysfunction. If Fox's slate featured "what're they doing here?" quality series like *The Tracey Ullman Show*, too, well, then they were there to keep the cops away.

With its id firmly in control, the network that snipers said could never work, worked. It carved out an identity as the young, frisky network for young, frisky viewers. It got rich off

of stuff that the Big Three previously wouldn't have deigned worthy of primetime real estate: *Married . . .*, the smart-mouthed *Simpsons*, the camcorder fare of *America's Most Wanted* and *World's Wildest Police Chases*. And, in fairness, it took chances on stuff that the Big Three wouldn't have touched—the serious-minded black comedy *Roc*, the out-there *Ben Stiller Show*, the unusually un-stupid *It's Garry Shandling's Show* (a pickup from cable's Showtime). Somewhat a victim of its success, its more grown-up efforts didn't quite click with its short-attention-span lineup. *Bakersfield, P.D.* would come (and go); *Married . . . With Children* would stay (and stay). Hourlong successes, in particular, were in serious short supply. *The X-Files*—a UFO show that didn't make you feel silly about watching a UFO show—was Fox's shining exception. Critics liked it, the right demographic grouping of viewers liked it, Emmy voters liked it. It added up to that rarest of Fox trifectas: a series that was hip, hot *and* (what?!?) good. A pretty nice change of pace. It was (almost) enough to make you forget that Fox was still quite capable of giving Pauly Shore money to make a sitcom. (See: *Pauly*. On second thought, don't.)

Beverly Hills 90210, *Melrose Place* and, to a lesser degree, *Party of Five* were other long-form hits for the network, but they weren't taken as seriously. Rightly or wrongly (and mostly due to an overwhelming number of dimples), those series got discounted as kid shows. Fox was going to have to look elsewhere if it wanted another show to deliver attention *and* acclaim.

In an unlikely but logical TV-land scenario, the network found salvation through Amanda Woodward.

The *Melrose Place* Connection

Onscreen, *Ally McBeal* and *Melrose Place* seem to share little more than a network (Fox). One is artfully daffy; the other, unabashedly melodramatic. One is the Hot New Show; the other, the Cooling Aging Show. One is mostly good; the other, um, used to be. But in the spirit of fairness, let it be noted that *Ally* owes no small margin of its success to *MP*. Indeed, as *Ally* folklore tells us, its very existence was predicated on Fox's desire for a *MP* companion. The network could not have made a more sage choice in selecting *Ally* for the assignment. There exists between these two shows an almost eerie interconnectedness. The usual reasons for such sameness (the spin-off syndrome, chiefly) do not apply here. Indeed, it appears no less than The Fates have intervened. Consider:

The premise: *MP* is a show about a blonde, single woman (Heather Locklear's Amanda Woodward) who wears dangerously short skirts en route to forging a career as a successful professional. In her spare time, she shagged a guy named Billy (Andrew Shue). *Ally* is a show about a blonde, single woman (Calista Flockhart's Ally McBeal) who wears dangerously short skirts en route to forging a career as a successful young professional. In her youth, she shagged a guy named Billy (Gil Bellows).

The Courtney Thorne-Smith thing: On *MP*, Thorne-Smith played Alison Parker, a down-to-earth Wisconsin gal in a star-crossed relationship with a lovably dopey guy named Billy (yes, the same Billy as in Amanda's Billy). On *Ally*, Thorne-Smith plays Georgia Thomas, a down-to-earth Michigan gal in a sometimes-troubled relationship with a lovably dopey guy named Billy (yes, the same Billy as in Ally's Billy). To take this argument one step further, let it also be noted that "Ally" is the familiar form of "Alison," meaning that, like *MP*, *Ally* is dominated by the dynamics of a Billy-Alison relationship. (Thorne-Smith explained her take on the matter thusly, on *Late Night with Conan O'Brien*: "On *Melrose Place*, it was 'Billy! Billy!' [a whiny, scolding tone]. . . . And on *Ally*

McBeal, it's 'Billy. . . . Billy.' [an older, sadder tone]. It's a totally different name.")

The workplace thing: Amanda's advertising agency coworkers find her demanding, yet undeniably capable; Ally's law firm coworkers find her utterly loony, yet strangely capable.

The hangouts: After a hard day having sex with each other, the twentysomethings of *MP* cool their heels at a pool hall where popular music of their approximate generation is rarely played. After a hard day dawdling with each other in the unisex bathroom, the twentysomethings of *Ally* cool their heels at a bar where popular music of their approximate generation is never played.

Six degrees of *Ally*: *MP* is executive produced by Aaron Spelling, who executive-produced *Charlie's Angels* (1976–81), which starred Kate Jackson, who guest-starred on *Ally*'s Season No. 1 episode "The Kiss."

Family affair: On *Ally*, Dyan Cannon plays Judge Whipper Cone. Cannon's daughter is Jennifer Grant, who played Celeste, one of Ian Ziering's TV girlfriends on *Beverly Hills 90210*, which spawned, yes, *MP*.

Other assorted spooky things:

- *MP* featured a nut-job character named Kimberly Shaw (Marcia Cross) who, following a bad bump on the head, suffered delusional spells. *Ally* features several nut-job characters who, for no apparent medical reasons, suffer delusional spells.
- In 1994 (and 1995, 1996 and 1997), Heather Locklear was nominated for a Golden Globe for Outstanding Lead Actress in a Drama Series. In 1998, Calista Flockhart was nominated for (and won) a Golden Globe for Outstanding Lead Actress in a Comedy/Musical Series. Some would argue that neither actress was truly qualified for the category in which she competed.
- *MP* takes place in Los Angeles, California. *Ally* takes place in Boston, Massachusetts. Both are cities. Big ones. (Um, maybe it's time to cut off the list now before we start groping for stuff.)

In early 1997, the suits at Fox decided that Heather Locklear, the leggy vixen of its long-running *Melrose Place*, needed a friend. Even if the aging primetime soap wasn't the ratings dynamo or must-see camp classic of its media-saturated glory days, the melodrama about oversexed Los Angeles twentysomethings and the apartments they sleep (around) in could still deliver sponsor-friendly demographics: young women, ages eighteen to thirty-four, with money to spend and malleable ideas on how to spend it. Problem was, *MP*'s good work was being wasted. Since the series began anchoring Fox's Monday nights in the 1994–95 season, the network had unsuccessfully mixed-and-matched companion shows in the 9:00–10:00 P.M. follow-up time slots. Overt Generation X–pandering sitcoms like *Partners* and *Ned and Stacey* flopped. Even *Party of Five*, the weepy family drama with a loyal, if not expansive following, didn't match up with *MP*. For the sake of its survival, the fledgling show had to be shipped off (and quick) to Wednesdays, to work in tandem with *90210*.

This was not good. With Amanda Woodward's charms on the decline, Fox needed a fix—and fast. If it was going to build on *MP*'s enviable audience, it had to do so before that audience was completely eroded.

For a change, the network passed up a chance to commission a new Aaron Spelling–style soap, and instead put out a call to producer David E. Kelley. The request: Pitch us a *Melrose*-friendly neighbor.

"We had a very singular point of view about the kind of show we wanted. We had a time slot in mind," Fox network president Peter Roth said at a Viewers for Quality Television

conference in 1997. "We gave [Kelley] as much freedom as is humanly possible."

All Kelley had to do was produce. Give Fox the sort of show that was Foxlike, only better. Give Fox a show that would produce *MP*-style ratings, only better.

No problem.

Chapter 4
That Lawyer Guy

Once, David E. Kelley was a young lawyer as conflicted and tormented as Ally McBeal on a good day. He was in his late twenties. He was a graduate of Princeton University and Boston University Law School. He was an associate member of a prestigious Bay State firm. He was a young man with a future—which he didn't want.

Kelley was born in 1956 in Maine—approximately (rough estimate) one million miles from Hollywood. The future TV mogul was no Quentin Tarantino, a robo-film-maker schooled on story structure and character development via the video store.

To hear Kelley tell it, as a kid he wasn't all that star-struck and wasn't even much of a writer. "[Although] some of my high school teachers did remind me that I had an excellent imagination when it came to making up excuses," he said in the *New York Times* in 1990.

Kelley's MO is to downplay, downplay, downplay. He *just happened* into a Hollywood career. *Just happened* to write (rough estimate) five hundred TV scripts in a single season. *Just happened* to get three shows up and running in primetime at the same time.

CHARGED WITH CREATING A *MELROSE PLACE* COMPANION SERIES, DAVID
E. KELLEY CRAFTED THE OFF-KILTER *ALLY MCBEAL*.
© ALBERT L. ORTEGA/FLOWER CHILDREN LTD.

Uh-huh. Consider Kelley's public posture of modesty
his gift to you: He doesn't want to make you feel any crappier
about your life. (Of course, if he *really* cared, he wouldn't have
married Michelle Pfeiffer, too. But nobody—not even David
E. Kelley—is perfect.)

In any case, about the most authorly ambitions Kelley
will cop to are some comedy sketches he wrote at Princeton.
Other than that lapse, he remained focused on a career in law.
Until he got a real taste of a career in law.

The ordeal began in 1983, when he joined Boston's Fine
and Ambrogne. The firm was great, the powers-that-be were
great, the other lawyers—great. One problem: It was "every
bit as boring as one could imagine a law career being," he told
TV Guide.

Struck with an idea for a movie, Kelley decided to write a screenplay. In his spare time, the unconventional young lawyer and avowed Hollywood novice scribbled—in long-hand, on yellow legal pads—a movie script about (what else?) an unconventional young lawyer.

It *just happened* to sell.

So as not to overplay Kelley's golden hand, let it be noted that the script didn't actually sell for another three years. In 1986, he was still arguing writs and habeas corpi and other arcane Latin theories when he secured an agent (schmoozing a friend for a connection). His long-ago movie script finally made the rounds and, in short order, scored an enviable twofer: It got bought (transformed into the regrettable 1987 comedy *From the Hip*, starring future *Suddenly Susan* inmate Judd Nelson) and it got attention. Chiefly, it got the attention of Steven Bochco, who (yes) *just happened* to be looking for writers with legal expertise. Bochco was the mythic producer whom critics loved to celebrate for supposedly rescuing TV drama from the moribund, cookie-cutter likes of *Barnaby Jones*. Bochco's answer to bang-bang cop shows was kiss-kiss-bang-bang cop shows. With sex and TV-land grit and women and gallows humor, he transformed *The Rookies* into *Hill Street Blues*. He made primetime an unsafe place for the unhip. If Angela Lansbury's looking for someone to blame for (*rough* estimate) a thousand Emmy nominations and zero wins, she can look to Steven Bochco. After *Hill Street*, if you weren't on a Bochconian series, you were nowhere—you were just a schlep with a paycheck, a TV show and a mission to serve shut-ins and rest-home residents. Bochco's cool was the

only cool. And when Bochco said you were cool, you were cool. He said David E. Kelley was cool.

Kelley was brought on board to write for Bochco's new lawyer series: *L.A. Law*. The series, about a skyscraperful of La-La Land attorneys, their fancy suits and Harry Hamlin's pout, premiered on NBC on September 15, 1986. At first, Kelley played it safe, maintaining his law job while cranking out *Law* scripts. Healthy ratings and big-time Emmy wins made it clear *Law* wasn't going anywhere anytime soon. Kelley moved west after the first season. By 1988, he was the show's supervising producer. By 1989, he was Bochco's hand-picked successor as executive producer. Appropriately, his first season out of the box, *Law* won the Emmy for Outstanding Drama Series. His second season out of the box? *Law* won the Emmy for Outstanding Drama Series. (The series had previously won for the 1986–87 and 1988–89 TV years, too.) Under his tenure, he introduced the notoriously icy Rosalind Shays (played by Diana Muldaur—in an older precursor of future *Ally* associate Nelle Porter), and the sexually uninhibited C. J. Lamb (Amanda Donohoe—in a precursor to just about everybody on *Ally*). Displaying a knack for timing as well as screenplays, he got out while the getting was mostly good, leaving the suddenly floundering *Law* in 1992. (The show was finally put down in 1994.)

The same year Kelley ascended to executive producer on *Law*, he also teamed with Bochco to create his first series, *Doogie Howser, M.D.* The premise was every bit, if not more, preposterous than the notion of a top-drawer lawyer who dresses like a T.G.I.Fridays hottie. *Doogie* was about a sixteen-year-old doctor (Neil Patrick Harris) who maintained

AMONG OTHER ACCOMPLISHMENTS, DAVID E. KELLEY *JUST HAPPENS* TO BE
MARRIED TO MOVIE STAR MICHELLE PFEIFFER.
© SUE SCHNEIDER/FLOWER CHILDREN LTD.

healthy, like-age friendships, dated and enjoyed a fairly
unblemished complexion. (Frankly, the show was about as
preposterous as Kelley's touched-by-an-angel career.) The
half-hour "dramedy"—part comedy, part drama, no laugh
track—ran on ABC from 1989 to 1993.

On November 13, 1993, Kelley wed one-time Oscar-
nominee and full-time A-list movie star Michelle Pfeiffer
(*The Fabulous Baker Boys*, *Scarface*).

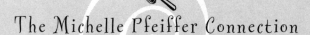

The Michelle Pfeiffer Connection

"Movie Beauty Is Inspiration for Zany TV Show.". . . Well, if the *Star* prints it, it must be true.

Oh, sure, David E. Kelley often has dismissed the notion that he mines his domestic life, in general, and his famed spouse, in specific, for series material. His wife, actress Michelle Pfeiffer, is *not* Ally McBeal, he says; he did *not* cast Calista Flockhart because she resembled Michelle Pfeiffer, he protests.

Fine. Whatever. Let the evidence be our guide:

The name thing: Michelle Pfeiffer's name is sixteen letters long; Calista Flockhart's name is . . . *sixteen letters long*!

The gender thing: Michelle Pfeiffer is a woman; Calista Flockhart is . . . *a woman*!

The horoscope thing: Michelle Pfeiffer (born April 29) is a Taurus, the bull; Calista Flockhart (born November 11) is a Scorpio, the scorpion . . . *the natural animal-kingdom pal of the bull!* (All right, we're making that one up.)

The mommy thing: Michelle Pfeiffer is the mother of two children; Calista Flockhart mothers a dog, name of Webster.

The Peter Horton thing: Michelle Pfeiffer once was married to actor Peter Horton (*thirtysomething*); Calista Flockhart costars on *Ally* with Peter MacNicol, who once costarred with Meryl Streep (*Sophie's Choice*), who once costarred with Kevin Bacon (*The River Wild*), who costarred with wife Kyra Sedgwick (*Murder in the First*), who once costarred with . . . Peter Horton (*Singles*)!

The hard-luck story: Proto-actress Michelle Pfeiffer once toiled as a checkout clerk at a Vons supermarket in Orange County, California; struggling actress Calista Flockhart once subsisted on canned ravioli, the likes of which can be purchased at . . . *Vons*!

The early indignities: The powers-that-be misspelled Michelle Pfeiffer's name ("Michele") in the credits of her 1978 TV series, *Delta House*; the powers-that-be offered Calista Flockhart day work on New York–based soap operas.

The big break: Michelle Pfeiffer played Al Pacino's girlfriend in *Scarface* (1993); Calista Flockhart played Dan Futterman's girlfriend in *The Birdcage* (1996), which costarred Gene Hackman, who appeared in *Scarecrow* (1973) with . . . *Al Pacino*!

MICHELLE PFEIFFER.
© ALBERT L. ORTEGA/FLOWER CHILDREN LTD.

The *People* tributes: Michelle Pfeiffer was named one of the magazine's 50 Most Beautiful People (1990–91); Calista Flockhart was named one of the magazine's 50 Most Beautiful People (1998).

The music thing: Michelle Pfeiffer appeared in a music video for warmed-over rapper Coolio ("Gangsta's Paradise," from her film *Dangerous Minds*); Calista Flockhart appeared in a music video for warmed-over singer Vonda Shepard ("Searchin' My Soul").

CALISTA FLOCKHART.
© JEAN CUMMINGS/FLOWER CHILDREN LTD.

The Shakespeare thing: Michelle Pfeiffer plays Titania in the upcoming big-screen retelling of *A Midsummer Night's Dream*; Calista Flockhart plays Helena in the upcoming big-screen retelling of . . . *A Midsummer Night's Dream*!

The bottom line: In real life, Michelle Pfeiffer appears to be a stable individual not prone to wigging-out on a weekly basis; on TV, Calista Flockhart's Ally McBeal, um, doesn't.

On the work front, he moved on to his first solo, hour-long outing, *Picket Fences*. The Emmy-winning CBS series, starring Tom Skerritt and Kathy Baker as upstanding citizens of the fictional Rome, Wisconsin, premiered on September 18, 1992. It was weird, it was quirky, it was populated by odd-ball legal types (notably, Ray Walston's Judge Bone). It wasn't quite *Ally*, but it was getting there.

Chicago Hope—yet another Kelley production—also was known to be in touch with its quirky side. It even was known to employ Peter MacNicol. In the 1994–95 season (the CBS medical drama's inaugural TV year), Kelley cranked out more than a combined forty scripts for *Picket Fences* and *Chicago Hope*. Because he still eschewed typing for longhand scrawl, carpal tunnel wasn't an issue. Unfortunately, TV overload was. Even the guy who liked to maintain that *everything* was effort-less couldn't shrug off that grind. He left the two series in 1995—to, arguably, the detriment of both. (*Picket Fences* went off the air in 1996; *Chicago Hope* marked its one-hundredth episode in October 1998, amid public griping from stars Christine Lahti and Peter Berg about the show's quality.)

After a brief foray in film (as screenwriter on *To Gillian, On Her 37th Birthday*, costarring Pfeiffer), Kelley got back into the primetime way. *The Practice*, launched on ABC in the winter of 1997, was his first at-length return to the TV legal profession since *Law*. A conventional, story-driven lawyer show, Kelley still saw it as the flip side to the conventional, story-driven *Law*.

"I wanted to create characters who still clung to the ide-alism of what law could be," he said in *USA Today*.

Kelley's vision of idealism translated into a dead-serious show starring dead-serious Dylan McDermott as top dog of a low-rent Boston firm. Like *Picket Fences*, it was a critical hit and a ratings nonentity. *Chicago Hope* was his most Nielsen-approved series—and the one with which he had the least long-term involvement.

Bochco's genius had been to make *Hill Street Blues* and *L.A. Law* beloved not only by the TV intelligentsia (such as it was), but important to everyday civilians—the fans who hashed out the previous night's primetime offerings over lunch at the office. Kelley was a human scriptwriting machine, but was anybody *really* paying attention? The late NBC executive Brandon Tartikoff used to have a saying about comedian Steve Allen, the original *Tonight Show* host and would-be music great: "The guy says he wrote [*rough estimate*] one million songs. . . . Name one."

David E. Kelley needed The One—the signature hit.

Then he *just happened* upon *Ally*.

Chapter 5
Finding Ally

When singer Vonda Shepard first heard about David E. Kelley's new idea for a series, the concept was a bit muddy— at least in her mind. "At one point it was a lawyers show and another time a sitcom, so I wasn't sure if it was going to be a musical-lawyers series or what," Shepard told *TVGen*.

As it turned out, Kelley's grand scheme combined all three elements: the lawyer show, the sitcom (well, comedy) and music—lots of music.

In response to Fox's request for a series to hang with *Melrose Place*'s youngish female viewership, Kelley cooked up a concoction about a youngish female lawyer. Rather, it was about a youngish female who *just happened* to be a lawyer. (Technically, his first pitch to the network had been for an hourlong series about a parson's wife called *The Parson's Wife*. Didn't fly. Trying to sell Fox on a church show was like trying to bring little Damien from *The Omen* to Sunday mass.)

The lawyer show was to be by turns dramatic, funny, sexy (always a good bet to pique the interest of the Foxies) and farcical. Above all, its stories were to be told from the young woman's point of view. Granted, the young woman's point of view was coming straight from the pen of an XY-chromosome

human, but that was a minor quibble. In Hollywood, you're an expert on something the second you say you're on expert on something—*anything*. Did you have to be stranded on a desert island with a gaggle of morons to write *Gilligan's Island*? Did you have to be a Federation member to draft *Star Trek* assignments for Captain Kirk? Of course not. You just had be able to make it up. Kelley could make it up. In a sincere sort of way.

If you're doing a show named *Ally McBeal*, you better find the *right* Ally McBeal. Kelley and company needed an actress with whom an audience could share close quarters. Kelley needed an actress who would bring audiences into Ally's head, not hold them at length in a jury box. And, most importantly, Kelley needed an actress who wouldn't make Ally really, really annoying. (Slightly annoying, on the other hand, was acceptable—and welcomed.)

His first choice for the gig, he told *Entertainment Weekly*, was Bridget Fonda. The daughter of *Easy Rider* icon Peter Fonda, niece of "Hanoi Jane" icon Jane Fonda, and granddaughter of *Grapes of Wrath* icon Henry Fonda, Bridget Fonda is a winsome, appealing actress with some nice credits (*It Could Happen to You*, *Singles*, *Jackie Brown*) and an as-yet non-iconic career—unless you count her longtime (and now defunct) couplehood status with fellow Gen X actor (and future *Chicago Hope* costar) Eric Stoltz (which you don't). As it turned out, Fonda was not to achieve icon status through *Ally McBeal*. Talks didn't go anywhere. Back to square one.

Square one was not a fun place to be. In fact, it was a frustrating place to be. The *Ally* people couldn't find Ally.

They saw actress after actress after actress. Some were good, some quite good—none right.

Enter Calista Flockhart.

There's something of a love story to the successful Hollywood casting session: i.e., "Our eyes met; violins played; I knew he/she was the one for me." The *Ally* people were no less star-struck by Flockhart, a thirtysomething Broadway actress (*The Glass Menagerie*) whom they'd long lobbied to read for the part. Turned out the arrival of the woman with the funny name was worth the wait.

"When she came in, we just knew," series co-executive producer Jeffrey Kramer said at a Viewers for Quality Television conference in 1997. "It just happens sometimes, and it's truly the right person in the right role at the right time."

Indeed, Flockhart seemed to have a clear take on the character—clearer than most pundits—once describing Ally to the *Los Angeles Times' TV Times* as "a kid who goes into a room filled with junk, certain there's a pony inside. And she's determined to find it."

New York–based Flockhart was loath to move to Hollywood and take on a primetime series. But it's hard to say no to nice people who offer you a nice job with nice pay. Flockhart was human. She took it. Kelley had his Ally. Flockhart had her shot at icon status.

Bridget Fonda had her peace of mind.

The other *Ally* players were culled largely from Flockhart's ranks of the middling-to-hardly famous. Gil Bellows, slotted as nice-guy Billy, was a theater vet whose biggest movie role

THE *ALLY MCBEAL* CAST—MINUS ALLY MCBEAL—AT THE 1998 GOLDEN
GLOBE AWARDS. FRONT ROW, LEFT TO RIGHT: LISA NICOLE CARSON, JANE
KRAKOWSKI. BACK ROW, LEFT TO RIGHT: GIL BELLOWS, GREG GERMANN,
COURTNEY THORNE-SMITH, PETER MACNICOL, VONDA SHEPARD.
© SUE SCHNEIDER/FLOWER CHILDREN LTD.

to date was in a Sarah Jessica Parker vehicle (*Miami Rhapsody*), which is a lot like having your biggest movie role come in, say, a Rhea Perlman vehicle. The part may be swell. The picture may be great. The audience will be small.

Greg Germann, cast as Fish, was a survivor of Fox's *Ned and Stacey*. Jane Krakowski, tapped as secretary Elaine, was a scene-stealer of musical-theater note (*Grand Hotel*, *Once Upon a Mattress*).

Lisa Nicole Carson, pegged as Renee, was probably the most recognizable of the bunch, with a recurring role on the top-rated *ER* and a notable turn in the Denzel Washington movie *Devil in a Blue Dress*.

Rounding out the cast for the pilot was Anna Gunn as Billy's wife Georgia. Gunn was a TV actress who had guested on Kelley's *Chicago Hope* and claimed a regular series role on the forgettable Fox hormone comedy *Down the Shore* (1992). (Thorne-Smith and MacNicol's days were yet to come.)

The final addition to the on-air team was Vonda Shepard—another middling-to-hardly famous person with a professional résumé (three solo albums, one Top Ten single) and a thoroughly unhappening career. Unlike the others, her specialty was singing and songwriting, not acting. Why Kelley would need the services of a former Jackson Browne backup was unclear—mostly to Shepard. But, again, it's hard to say no to nice people who offer you a nice job with nice pay. If Kelley thought his lawyer series needed (what else?) a house singer, then so be it. If Kelley thought his lawyer series needed Shepard's voice (not to mention her songs), then so be it. Bopping around nightclub to nightclub was fun for just so long. But a primetime TV series? Bring it on.

Chapter 6
Making TV

The time came for David E. Kelley to turn in his *Ally* drafts to Fox. Next, he figured, came the time for Fox to tell him no.

As in, "No, you can't say this." Or, "No, you can't show this." Or, "No, Ally McBeal can't *be* this." Or the all-purpose "No, no, no."

But, as Kelley told *Entertainment Weekly*, the big "No" never came. This was, after all, Fox—home of *When Good Pets Go Bad*. Kelley was going to have to come up with something a little more scurrilous than literate-minded scripts that, for kicks, called for giant, hit-the-floor tongues and cappuccino-foam lip-licking. Maybe those stunts would give the old guard at CBS the creeps. At Fox? Hey, the more tongues the merrier. Skirts? Make 'em shorter! Go ahead—live it up! Swing, baby!

The bottom line: *Ally* was a go.

The key: *Ally*, as envisioned by Kelley, was a go.

The chick show written, conceived and produced by a guy, was about to happen.

Let the debates begin.

Good TV is, often, difficult TV. You knock off a *Family Matters*. You suffer for a *Moonlighting*. To be sure, there were

no anarchic stories of Bruce-and-Cybill proportions to emanate from the *Ally* set. But they did abide by an exacting sense of detail common to high-maintenance, overachieving series.

Except for the scripts—which Kelley swore he virtually jotted down in two modest, 9:00 A.M.–to–6:00 P.M. workdays each week (the better not to interfere with his jotting-down sessions for *The Practice*, which he also largely wrote)—the series was a backbreaker.

Shoot days lasted into the teens—as in fourteen, fifteen, seventeen hours long. Entire episodes ate up nine to eleven production days, as opposed to the usual seven- to eight-day schedules. Post-production, thanks to those hit-the-floor–tongues special effects, required almost thirty days instead of the usual twenty-one. "Quality," Kelley said in *TV Guide*, "takes time."

The tinkering never let up—from reshoots to new shoots. Scenes and characters never noted in a script were added in a heartbeat. Scenes and characters dutifully noted in a script were deleted in a second heartbeat. None of this was unusual for a network series, but none of this was insignificant, either.

Tinkering cost Anna Gunn her job. The story goes that Kelley initially conceived the Georgia Thomas role as minor—apparently making Gunn perfect. When he reconceived the role as being sort of major, Gunn apparently was no longer perfect. The services of a new actress were required. That the new actress, Courtney Thorne-Smith, *just happened* to be an alumnus from key lead-in *Melrose Place* was—well, you know . . . just one of those things.

Thorne-Smith joined the cast after the first version of the pilot was in the can. Her first order of business was, obviously, to reshoot the Georgia scenes.

"My first day, I came in late. So I felt everyone knew each other and it was my first day at a new school," Thorne-Smith told *Entertainment Tonight Online*.

And because this was *Ally*, not *Moonlighting*, everyone played nice.

The music component was another work-in-progress. Kelley hired Vonda Shepard to serve as Ally's "musical conscience," Shepard told CNN. "I'm her Greek chorus, her inner thoughts."

The question was, what were those inner thoughts going to sound like?

Since Shepard was around, the easy first answer was: A lot like a blandly pleasant VH-1 artist. Now, this isn't a *mean* answer. Many blandly pleasant VH-1 artists are, after all, very successful. And their success? The direct result of their— yes—blandly pleasant sound. (Long live Matchbox 20!) Besides, the most important thing was Kelley liked Shepard's sound—blandly pleasant or no—and he was the boss. She was the Greek chorus.

"Basically, I just read the script, and I get the feeling of a scene," Shepard told Reuters News Service, of their working arrangement. "Then I'll maybe do something with a little more sadness or something uptempo, whatever is called for."

Shepard, being a singer/songwriter, first suggested her own catalog of material. Kelley okayed more than a dozen of

her picks—right down to borrowing her 1992 cut, "Searchin' My Soul," for the series' theme song.

But baby boomer Kelley—being as much an authentic voice on women as he was an authentic voice of modern-day twentysomethings—had a notion that many of Ally McBeal's thoughts sounded a lot like AM radio from the early 1970s. Hence, he asked Shepard, not accustomed to playing the cover-friendly lounge artist, to play the cover-friendly lounge artist. In short time, she was crooning oldies like "Don't Walk Away Renee," "The End of the World," and "Tell Him."

It worked for *The Big Chill*. It could (and did) work for *Ally*.

If there was one element of the early *Ally* that didn't need a lot of work, it was Ally herself. Flockhart was nailing it. Voice-overs, so frequent and obvious in the first episodes, grew less frequent as producers decided Flockhart was doing a good enough job expressing the inner thoughts of their resident wack job on her own. In her hands (or lips), a simple bit on paper—a judge asking Ally to show him her teeth—became a major comedy bit, with Flockhart's lips all atremble and aquiver.

"I sometimes feel like [Kelley] knew Calista in advance," Kramer said at the Viewers for Quality Television Conference. "I don't know who's leading who—Calista or the character or David. . . ."

Pretty soon, neither would the public.

A word about the skirts: From the onset, it was decided to costume Ms. Flockhart as Ms. McBeal in skirts that would barely qualify for hand-towel status. In the *New York Times*, a Fox spokeswoman defended the wardrobe as a character choice: "They want her to be intelligent, but they want her to be appealing, too."

Exactly.

Chapter 7
Love/Hate

It all came down to this: the *Ally McBeal* premiere.

The tailor-made, post–*Melrose Place* time slot was ready; the Fox hype machine was locked and loaded. On paper, the network sold staid, respectable stuff like, "a new one-hour series from one of television's most celebrated producers. . . ." On TV spots, it sold nonstop *yeah, baby*! stuff like the expandable-breast sequence. As always, Fox wanted attention and acclaim.

Ally gave the network all that. *Ally* gave its cast all that.

Ally gave till it hurt.

The first Kelley-drafted episode to make it to air was entitled simply, "Pilot." It introduced his quirky heroine and her quirky so-called life: Girl (Ally) follows boy (childhood love Billy) to law school; boy transfers; girl grows up to become an attorney; girl joins Boston firm; girl gets groped by senior partner; girl quits firm; girl bumps into old classmate (Fish); old classmate offers girl job at his law firm; girl accepts; girl learns boy works at same firm; girl discovers she's still stuck on boy; boy tells girl he's married. Oh, boy.

In the weeks to follow, the series followed Ally's girllike need to find a boy; Billy's boylike need to keep Ally faraway—and close; Fish's obsessive need to make money; and all the young lawyers' inexplicable need to blow off steam at an oldies-blasting meat-market nightclub.

The flashiest conceit of the new show was its special effects. In case anyone tried to ding Kelley for putting over a rehash of *L.A. Law* or *The Practice*, he made sure *Ally* was TV's first-ever legal series to feature its lead lawyer imagining herself in triplicate—the better to duplicate Gladys Knight's Pips. (Long story. Best explained upon viewing of the Season No. 1 episode "The Playing Field.")

Ally, it was clear, was a character who was out of her mind, inhabiting a show that was all but out of its mind.

TV critics—their expectations lowered, their brains numbed by one *Single Guy* too many—generally were out of their minds in praise of Kelley's new show:

> "It is fast-paced, funny, touching, romantic and surprising." (Terry Kellcher, *People*)

> ". . . Refreshing and offbeat." (Caryn James, *The New York Times*)

> ". . . One of the season's best . . . with a shot at true excellence within its reach." (David Bianculli, *New York Daily News*)

> "Funny, endearing, intelligent and sexy." (Susan Young, *Oakland Tribune*)

> ". . . Sparkles with humanity, wit and promise." (Phil Kloer, *Atlanta Journal-Constitution*)

WHO HER? YES, HER—CALISTA FLOCKHART, AKA TV'S REVILED/REVERED
ALLY MCBEAL, PLAYING INNOCENT FOR CAMERAS.
© ALBERT L. ORTEGA/FLOWER CHILDREN LTD.

The list of raves was pretty long. Fox posted an assortment on its *Ally* Web site on the off-chance any civilian party
was interested. Fox certainly was (and is). Acceptance like
that (almost) made up for a million *Paulys*.

In the spirit of full disclosure, it should be noted that not
all initial reviews were brimming with falling-over admira-

tion. *TV Guide*'s Jeff Jarvis thought the show promising ("Everything I want in a series"), but remained suspicious of Kelley's intentions ("my most and least favorite producer—most favorite because he makes great TV . . . least favorite because he deserts his shows and lets them shrivel."). Howard Rosenberg of the *Los Angeles Times* found *Ally* outright wanting ("Carefree—and flimsy").

But the overall vibe was positive. *Ally*, the critics said, was a show that aspired to the sublime. Flockhart, the critics said, was an actress that qualified as a true find. Her character was a little annoying sometimes, they allowed, but that was part of the program's charm.

Mark the phrase: a *little* annoying.

The other group to weigh in with their verdicts were viewers. Intrigued by the promos, incited by the reviews, they tuned in. En masse. Supposedly riding the coattails of *Melrose Place*, *Ally*'s series opener outdrew its elder—a 9.3 to an 8.6, in the top forty TV markets. (Each rating point represented 980,000 TV homes.) It was the best-performing Fox series in the 9:00–10:00 P.M. time slot since an *Alien Nation* episode in 1989. And when you start breaking records set by *Alien Nation*, can world domination be far behind? In a truer sign of things to come, the chick lineup (*MP*, *Ally*) more than held its own against the dude lineup (ABC's *Monday Night Football*), placing a close second.

The above was all evidence to support the "Love" portion of the subhead. Now, on to the "Hate."

Entertainment Weekly once described Ally McBeal as the sort of character who, like her spiritual TV godmother—single girl Mary Richards (of *The Mary Tyler Moore Show*)—could turn the world on with her smile—*if she wanted to.*

From the pilot, it was clear that Kelley's Ally didn't really want to. She had too many corners to be a sunny Mary clone. This was a self-involved, sometimes selfish woman—willing, in the way that TV heroes and heroines seldom are, to incur the moral indignation of the masses. Beyond-reproach Mary Richards, after all, would never yearn to bed an ex-boyfriend after finding out he's married. But Ally McBeal would. She wasn't perfect. A sin for which her portrayer and her creator would pay in a thousand op-ed pieces.

It took a few months for *Ally*'s "little" annoying qualities to grate full-time. Shortly after the premiere, the series went on a monthlong, baseball-induced hiatus—hardly enough exposure for The Thinkers to know for sure if it was worth launching a full-on bellyaching campaign. But then, from Halloween to Christmas, with Peter MacNicol now added as a regular cast member, the show steamed ahead. And it let Ally be Ally. Big time.

She was getting into fights over potato chips (in "One Hundred Years Away"). Fantasizing about being lofted above the heads of full-dress rabbis ("The Attitude"). Getting bent out of shape by dirty jokes ("The Dirty Joke"). Still wearing Those Skirts. Still acting so—well, girlie.

Enough was enough, The Thinkers said. A November 1997 essay in (what else?) the *Ally*-loving *Time* magazine declared David E. Kelley's heroine "Woman of the Year." It was a false compliment—an excuse to discuss whether Ally McBeal was "lovable" or a "simpering drag." Ultimately, author James Collins found Flockhart fine, but declared her

Calista Flockhart:
Her Life as a Tabloid Harlot

Become a star, become tabloid fodder. It's the way of all celebrities—Calista Flockhart not only being no exception, but being a prime target. She's young, she's single, she's new. *Enquirer* minds want to know: Who's she zooming? The supermarket press rarely, if ever, is at a loss for an answer. Here were some of the tabs' romantic theories from the *Ally* star's 1997–98 TV year:

Cedric Harris: This New York stage actor accompanied Flockhart to the 1998 Golden Globes. Mark that: He *accompanied* her. Of course, in the *National Enquirer*, Mr. Harris's role was portrayed as being a little more profound than that of escort. He was described as Flockhart's "hot new romance." Why, there was even talk of marriage and, yes, kids! The reaction from the happy "couple"? "We laughed," Flockhart told *Us*. "Heartily."

Garry Shandling: This would-be romantic coupling can't be attributed to the tabs. The credit for this one actually goes to mainstream reporters who thought they detected a spark between the neurotic comic (*The Larry Sanders Show*) and TV's neurotic Ally McBeal at the July 1998 Television Critics Association awards. There, the story goes, Shandling hit on the tube star. ("That show really should have won," the *New York Daily News* had Shandling rambling, referring to how *Larry Sanders* topped *Ally* for best-comedy honors. "Calista Flockhart is the most talented. . . .You're single, right?") Later, TV-critic types spied the two huddling in the hotel bar. And *even later*, TV-critic types spied Flockhart slipping into Shandling's limo. . . . Unfortunately for fans of celeb couples, that was about all they wrote on the Shandling-Flockhart front.

Jeffrey Kramer: *Ally*'s co-executive producer was the subject of the most prolonged romance rumors. Months before Kramer's name surfaced, there

ACTOR CEDRIC HARRIS ACCOMPANIES
CALISTA FLOCKHART TO THE 1998 GOLDEN
GLOBE AWARDS, EN ROUTE TO BEING
DUBBED THE *ALLY* STAR'S "HOT NEW
ROMANCE."
© SUE SCHNEIDER/FLOWER CHILDREN LTD.

were whispers that Flockhart was dating a honcho from her series. This talk briefly ensnared the very-married David E. Kelley. But then the tabloids (sort of) cleared up the confusion: It wasn't Kelley that Flockhart was seeing. It was (supposedly) the show's *other* honcho, Kramer. The bespectacled producer (and former performer) shared a scene with Flockhart in the series pilot. The *National Enquirer* reported that the two loved to "watch videos of classic movies cuddled together on the couch." Cozy picture or no, the same article quoted no less than Kramer's estranged wife as noting that Jeffrey and Calista were just "friends." By the beginning of Season No. 2, the Kramer stories were history—replaced by the "Is Calista an anorexic?" headlines. And so the news cycle goes.

character something less-than-fine—the craven result of Fox's demographic desires, as if any primetime show was above craven demographic desires. (As if, say, Chuck Norris huddled with the writing staff of *Walker, Texas Ranger* and said: How can we make this *more real*?) Unless the show runs on Sunday mornings and stars Sam Donaldson, *every* network program is about what character appeals to who and why.

But the realities of show business were of no concern to people setting the headline type: "You Want to Slap Ally

McBeal, But Do You Like Her?" (*The New York Times*); "Giggle TV: Girls Are In, Women Out" (Associated Press); "Stepping Backward with Ally" (*The Baltimore Sun*); "TV's Ally McBeal wants to be the thinking man's sex kitten—if she only had a brain" (*GQ*). And, of course, the famous, "Is Feminism Dead?"

That Ally wasn't supposed to be perfect, wasn't supposed to be a role model, wasn't supposed to be a symbol, was lost entirely on The Thinkers who blamed the character for not being perfect, not being a role model and symbolizing the death of the self-assured woman.

Kelley could talk until he threatened to push his work-day past 6:00 P.M. ("The reality is that I . . . don't write [women] differently from men. I just write the characters," he told *USA Today*.) Flockhart could get snappish on a reporter. ("I am *not* Ally McBeal," she insisted to *TV Guide*.) Fine, whatever. Defending *Ally* was a fight they were never going to win because *Ally* was never going to be like TV's standard-bearer of acceptable hip: a Steven Bochco series.

Bochco heroes—from *Hill Street* to *L.A. Law* to *NYPD Blue*—were stoic and/or explosive professionals consumed by their professions. Sex, love and relationships were used to leaven the drama—not *be* the drama.

Above all, Bochco heroes were tough guys—even the girls. When Andy Sipowicz broke down on *NYPD Blue*, that supposedly meant something. When Ally McBeal broke down, that supposedly meant nothing. After all, Ally was *always* breaking down—maybe not in tears, but in a general basket-case way.

Her biggest crime? She was no Grace Van Owen: *L.A. Law*'s stern leading lady (as essayed by Susan Dey) wouldn't bore you with her every self-doubt. Her every spare fantasy. She was a Serious Career Woman.

And you know what? If Grace Van Owen top-lined *The Grace Van Owen Show*, the thing would be a big, fat bore. About the third time one of her voice-overs discussed the joys of lockjaw as a fashion look, or went over her anal-retentive mental notes for trial that morning, the novelty would be over. Viewers—maybe even The Thinkers—would *run* to Ally and strike a pleading pose: "Please, please! Oh, for one more of your silly, yet strangely cogent thoughts about the homeless and their relation to your outfits!"

Viewers accepted what social critics were unwilling to: that Ally McBeal was a lot more interesting than other characters on TV. She was kind of like them in a way that Dharma and/or Greg and/or Grace Van Owen never could be. She was a mostly-well-meaning, screwed-up woman. She was, in few words, kind of human.

And you didn't have to be a man or a woman to write her—you just had to be human. On that, David E. Kelley qualified.

Chapter 8

"It"

A look back at the new-show competition of the 1997–98 TV class is the surest way to see why *Ally* generated so much teeth-gnashing: What the hell else were people going to talk about?

Dellaventura? The all-new *Tony Danza Show*? The return of Maureen "Marcia Brady" McCormick (via ABC's *Teen Angel*)? The return of Tom (*The Stupids*) Arnold (via the WB's *The Tom Show*)? The return of James "Jim" Belushi (via ABC's *Total Security*)?

There were four shows—count 'em, four new shows—that seemed worthy of any ink, or prolonged viewer interest: *Jenny*, the NBC Jenny McCarthy vehicle; *Nothing Sacred*, the ABC priest-assailed priest drama; *Dharma & Greg*, ABC's glorified, nondenominational *Bridget Loves Bernie*; and *Ally McBeal*.

About a month into the season it became clear that MTV celeb Jenny McCarthy and her tongue were "Must-See TV" jokes, and that *Nothing Sacred* was nothing special. Granted, critics and viewer-watchdog groups loved Kevin Anderson's crusading man of the cloth, but it suffered from one little problem: Nobody else cared.

That left two shows with a pulse. *Dharma & Greg* and *Ally*.

Now, *Dharma & Greg* was cute, but it wasn't exactly a world-beater. It was not an innovator. And it was no more a top ten or top twenty hit than *Ally* was. (Although, to be fair, it *was* a top thirty show—a height *Ally* wouldn't regularly reach until Season No. 2.) The point is, it wasn't like people were rearranging their lives to watch *Dharma & Greg*. How long could the media hope to hold the public's attention with "Jenna Elfman this, Jenna Elfman that" stories?

The answer: The media didn't wait to find out. Oh, Ms. Elfman got her perks, got her covers, got her *Entertainment Tonight* time. But when given the choice between profiling a "nice" giggly sitcom and a show with a somewhat advanced TV-sex libido? No contest.

By default, *Ally* was tagged "It."

To be sure, all the hallmarks of "It"-dom were there: the catchphrases ("McBealisms," "Fishisms," "bygones"); the signature gimmicks (the wattles, the personal theme songs); the stuff that plain old got people talking (the big-penis guy episode, the faux–Janet Reno guest appearances); the silly controversy (the "dirty dozen" designation from a group outraged by the big-penis guy episode); the hyperintense Internet fan activity; the inevitable hit soundtrack; the intense interest in its stars—especially Flockhart. Who was she? Who did she date? What was the deal with her name? Was she related to Michelle Pfeiffer? Was she *really* like Ally McBeal? . . . And, hey, wasn't she just a *little bony*, huh?

The foot never came off the gas pedal. By the new year, *Ally* had become so strong, so spunky, as to make its time-slot

sibling—its very reason for being on Fox—look even more tired than usual. Where *Melrose Place* was concerned, Fox executives broached the concept of cancellation. (Not that they had the guts to go through with it.) Where *Ally McBeal* was concerned, they gushed. ("The best of broadcast network television in its intelligence, wit, artistry and widespread commercial appeal," network president Peter Roth said.)

And then, in the space of a week, the dead-solid proof of the *Ally* explosion. On January 5, 1998, the series returned from Christmas break with "Cro-Magnon," heretofore known as the "big-penis guy episode." Also known as the "Dancing Baby episode." Kelley and company, including guest stars Michael Easton (as Big-Penis Guy) and the Dancing Baby (as the Dancing Baby), were on such a roll they couldn't even space out the water-cooler fodder. The episode was jam-packed with moments guaranteed to leave *Entertainment Weekly* subscribers pinching themselves in disbelief of their good fortune: "Is this a hot show, or what? Look at them funny lawyer people—they're talking penis sizes!" (In the best tradition of TV sex, *talk* is all they do.)

"And, hey, look at that funny lawyer lady—she's wearing really cute jammies and dancing with a really cute computer-animated baby!"

"Isn't this, like, *the best show ever!*"

The penis-and-baby-induced hysteria barely had subsided when (what's this!) magical Golden Globe night arrived.

There is no better test of an "It" show than the Golden Globes. The always-fun Hollywood Foreign Press Association is much more in touch with the pop-culture zeitgeist than its sober Emmy counterparts. The Golden Globe

people love the new! They love the bright, pretty lights! They think Heather Locklear deserves kudos for her *Melrose Place* work . . . *just like you!*

In the scheme of things, of course, you have to be pretty desperate to actually label yourself a "Golden Globe winner." Or, even worse, a "Golden Globe nominee." (Why not just buy an ad in *Variety*: "No, I Never Did Win an Oscar or an Emmy"?)

But for the purposes of a freshman "It" show? The award is vital. If you can't make a showing at the Golden Globes, forget the Emmys, forget the next few more months of magazine covers—your time is just about up.

The big night was January 11, 1998. The place was the Beverly Hilton. And the pressure was on from the start: Burt Reynolds won. *Burt Reynolds won!* (A best-supporting movie-actor nod for *Boogie Nights*.) The Globies clearly were in one of those enthusiastic moods. Burt Reynolds was back—and the Golden Globes had him!

Could *Ally McBeal* match that vibe? Had hype of the show's remarkable first half-season resonated in Globie Land?

Yes, it had!

Winner! Calista Flockhart, named Outstanding Comedy Actress.

Winner! *Ally McBeal*, named Outstanding Comedy Series.

As David E. Kelley and crew made their way to the stage to accept the show award, the snubbed players of retiring "It" comedy *Seinfeld* made their way to the exit. When the Globes didn't want you, it really was time to leave.

Chapter 9

Postscript: Fall 1998

Two months into Season No. 2, *Ally McBeal*'s ratings are stronger than ever. (So strong, in fact, that they even *look* like strong ratings. They're no longer the sort of numbers that have to be crunched through a demographics calculator to impress. They're *right there*—securing the show its long-awaited place in the top twenty.) And the cast is bigger than ever (thanks to new additions Portia de Rossi as frosty attorney Nelle Porter and Lucy Liu as her even frostier client, Ling Woo). And the critical notices are as strong as ever ("Soph far, soph great"—*New York Daily News*). And even with new "It" contenders like *Felicity* around, interest in the show is as big as ever.

And yet the only real *Ally* topics are (still): Calista Flockhart; The Dress; her weight.

On one hand, it's nice to be mostly (and finally) done with the feminist-oriented dissertations. It's nice to watch cooler heads prevail. It's nice to see The Thinkers slowly accept, or concede, the point: Ally McBeal is a fake person of no likely harm to myself or my family.

On the other hand, the anorexia stuff is hardly better.

In fact, if anything, there was something noble, if dumb-headed, about arguing Ally McBeal's place in the New World Order. There was something terribly intrusive, and flat-out wrong, about virtually forcing Calista Flockhart onto an "I do too eat" media tour.

And there is something pointless about getting worked up into an indignant snit over either cause.

Does it stink to be Calista Flockhart in the fall of 1998? Yeah, sort of. Fame's one thing. Money's one thing. A relatively juicy TV script's one thing.

Having a reporter stare at the bones in your arms is another. Feeling obligated to explain the size (or lack thereof) of the bones in your arm, as went down in Flockhart's *People* magazine I'm-not-an-anorexic confessional, is yet another matter entirely.

And having to listen to Tori Spelling issue your most impassioned public defense? ("Before she was Ally McBeal, she was just as thin, and they never said anything," the young Ms. Spelling told *USA Today*.) Let's not even go there.

It's just a guess, but this stuff doesn't sound much fun. And what sounds even less fun, is that there's not a whole lot that even the most skilled Hollywood spinmeisters can do to stop the staring, stop the talk.

Because *Ally* is *Ally* is *Ally*.

And what's going on outside of the show is seemingly predestined to be more important than what's going on inside.

Part Two
The Cast

Chapter 10
The Nuclear Family

They are the center, the glue, the stars—the people with their names in the opening credits. (Well, except Vonda Shepard—until that situation was remedied in Season No. 2.) They get the magazine covers. The fans. The fame. (Count Vonda in there.) And, hopefully, some good perks, too.

CALISTA FLOCKHART
(ALLY MCBEAL)

The *TV Guide* writer noted Calista Flockhart sounded "battle weary." It was February 1998. *Ally McBeal* had been on the air for five months.

Its star was sounding "battle weary."

That's the Cliff's Notes version of the following story:

Calista Flockhart got into acting, presumably, to act. Calista Flockhart accepted the *Ally* job, presumably, to act—maybe even to see how the other half (or where actors are concerned, the other .01 percent) lives on fat network paychecks. It's a guess here, that Calista Flockhart didn't get into acting to

become a champion for women's rights, a vilified role model for working women, a spokesperson for her feminist generation or a proponent of the Audrey Hepburn body type.

But she got all that stuff—times ten. She got the David E. Kelley scripts, she got the whispers about her weight, she got the money (a reported $30,000–$40,000 an episode during Season No. 1), she got the whispers about her weight, she got the baggage, she got the whispers about her weight, she got the expectations, she got the whispers about her weight, she got the magazine covers, she got the whispers about her weight, she got the tabloid stories, she got the whispers about her weight, she got the autograph requests, she got the whispers about her weight, she got the bags of fan mail, she got the whispers about her weight, she got the Golden Globe, she got the whispers about her weight, she got the Emmy nomination, she got the heat.

She got the *screaming* whispers about her weight.

She got blindsided.

By fall of 1998, there were few greater sports in the TV nation than (1) guessing Flockhart's weight, and (2) guessing Flockhart's weight.

Enquirer minds wanted to know: Was she (*psst!*) anorexic?

A rude question? Hey, what's rude among public properties? Viewers adopted Flockhart as their newest A-list star. They helped put her on the cover of *Time* magazine. They *cared*.

Besides, *wasn't* she too skinny-looking?

People had asked the question before, of other allegedly too-thin types. Teri Hatcher (*Lois and Clark*), Tori Spelling

(*Beverly Hills 90210*) and Lara Flynn Boyle (*The Practice*) come to mind.

But speculation about Flockhart crushed them all. This was no idle, "Fonzie's dead!" urban-legend chatter. These were full-on headlines ("Walking a Thin Line on Ally's Weight") in full-on "real" newspapers.

This was the *Ally* experience in a nutshell: out of control.

From the start, the experience was "a bit surreal," Flockhart allowed in the *Los Angeles Times*.

CALISTA FLOCKHART DIDN'T HAVE MUCH TO SMILE ABOUT WHEN HER WEIGHT, OR REPUTED LACK THEREOF, BECAME A NATIONAL OBSESSION.
© ALBERT L. ORTEGA/FLOWER CHILDREN LTD.

"It took us all by surprise. No one was prepared for what happened," she said in the newspaper in September 1998.

And Flockhart—not just "no one"—was at ground zero when "what happened" happened.

Where Flockhart went, people watched. During a holiday visit to her parents in late 1997, she incited a gawk fest. "I was like, 'Oh, no. What's wrong with me?'" she said in *Gist TV*. "And my mother sort of gently pointed out: 'They recognize you.' I was kind of shocked."

Early in the *Ally* run, Flockhart could joke about having "finally arrived"—the initiation being a supermarket tabloid story about her supposed love life. But by the *Times* interview, she was talking about how *it* (the fame, the attention, the

notoriety) was no longer a laugh riot. Talking about how the stares—the nonstop stares—made it (uh-oh) difficult to eat at restaurants.

So, we're back to Flockhart and her dining habits again, are we?

Is this what it's like to be Boris Yeltsin? To be poked and prodded about your health, every second of every day?

It's worse.

Boris Yeltsin lives in Russia where supermarkets, much less supermarket tabloids, are nonfactors.

The national economy aside, Yeltsin's got it easy.

Try being Calista Flockhart.

She was born November 11, 1964, in Freeport, Illinois, according to one biography. Unless she was born on November 11, 1965, in Iowa, according to another.

Pick a year, any year: 1963, 1964, 1965, whatever. Calista Flockhart, who cops to hoarding her privacy "psychotically," doesn't talk birthdays or birthdates. During *Ally*'s breakout season, she was variously listed as thirty-one, thirty-two, thirty-three and thirty-four. The nation's newspaper of record, the *New York Times*, pegged her at twenty-eight. Flockhart didn't like being pegged. Her age was as fluid as her early home life. She was one of those kids who blew through schools—a frequent flier of the interstate. Father Ronald was an executive with Kraft Foods. The corporate ladder required a lot of steps, and states—Illinois, Iowa, Minnesota, New Jersey. His family—wife, Kay, a schoolteacher, and two kids (son Gary and daughter Calista)—trudged across the country with him.

"Whenever you move, I think you lose your history," Flockhart said in *Us*.

And no small bit of your identity, too.

As a child, Flockhart wanted to lose one very particular part of her identity: her first name. Calista. It stuck out in the schoolyard.

Made people gawk.

Flockhart dreamed of being something more blendable—an Ann, a Jennifer. Anything but a Calista.

In the end, Flockhart stuck it out—and the name (her grandmother's—a Greek moniker meaning "most beautiful") stuck. And eventually so did she. In one place. The family (finally) settled down. Flockhart spent her high school and college years in New Jersey—first at Shawnee High in Medford, then at Rutgers University.

In high school, she was a cheerleader. An emotional one. She'd cry after losses. She took that emotion to Rutgers, channeled it and pursued drama—not the first major you'd pick for someone who didn't like to stand out.

In college, she appeared in school plays—including one production in which the *Star* tabloid was kind enough to point out, she was told: "YOU CAN'T ACT." (That was the frothing-at-the-mouth *Star* headline. The text of the review was a tad more reserved. Something along the lines of how Flockhart "did not reach the level of credibility" of her fellow actors.)

In the end, Flockhart stuck it out. She was going to be an actress.

She hit New York after Rutgers and saw her résumé grow exponentially: She worked at a health club, nabbed day-

player bits on the daytime soaps and built a rep as a stage actress.

In 1992, she made her first real coast-to-coast impression in an installment of the HBO series *Lifestories: Families in Crisis*. Flockhart carried the title role in the episode, "The Secret Life of Mary-Margaret: Portrait of a Bulimic." The twentysomething actress with the boyish noncurves played (uh-oh) a teenager beset by an eating disorder.

In retrospect, it probably wasn't the greatest career move for a woman who later would be asked to defend her ability to hold down food. But the critics seemed to like it. "A stunning performance," the *Los Angeles Times* said.

TV exposure or no, Flockhart was in no hurry to go Hollywood. Even if demi-legend had it that, in New York, she was drawing a $400 weekly Off-Broadway paycheck and subsisting on a case of canned ravioli purchased in a mercy mission by her older brother.

No matter, Flockhart stuck it out—she stayed based in New York. The routine became something like this: She'd freelance in the movies (*Drunks*, *Quiz Show*); she'd return to the theater. Onstage, she was growing into the biggest roles of her career—including the lonely and wan Laura Wingfield of Tennessee Williams's *The Glass Menagerie*. In 1994, she did *Menagerie* on Broadway opposite idol Julie Harris. Life in New York was getting better. But theater success had a price—it brought more tempting offers from Hollywood. And so the circle spun.

A turn in the Off-Broadway play *The Loop* (also from 1994) caught the eye of director Mike Nichols (*The Graduate*). He scouted her for his upcoming comedy, *The*

Birdcage, with Robin Williams and Nathan Lane. Flockhart was cast as ingenue Barbara Keeley, the sweet daughter of a United States senator (Gene Hackman) about to marry a sweet guy (Dan Futterman) who just happens to have been parented by a gay male couple (Williams and Lane). With her hair schoolgirl-long and her mood set on demure, Flockhart pulled off yet another teenage character, even as she was pushing (or was it steaming past?) thirty.

It would take Joe Eszterhas, the manly man, über-screenwriter of *Showgirls* infamy, to write Flockhart her first substantial film role. In *Telling Lies in America*, released a month after *Ally*'s September 1997 premiere, but lensed before the series went into production, Flockhart got to try her hand at a real live, postadolescent character and leave the dreamy teenage stuff to a real teenager, Brad Renfro (*The Client*). The uncharacteristically low-key and sincere Eszterhas film was a coming-of-age tale set in the rock 'n' roll Cleveland of the early 1960s. Renfro played a young Hungarian immigrant bewitched (and eventually burned) by two embodiments of his American ideal—a slick-talking deejay (Kevin Bacon) and an older woman (Flockhart). Flockhart's performance was measured, sad and likely a revelation to the millions who soon would know her for nothing but her flummoxing *Ally* ways.

But, ultimately, film had no greater hold on her than TV did. In February 1997, she bowed in Broadway's *Three Sisters*. The production was Chekhov as interpreted by youngish Hollywood: Lili Taylor (*I Shot Andy Warhol*), Eric Stoltz (*Pulp Fiction*), Billy Crudup (*Without Limits*). Add to the mix Amy Irving (the ex–Mrs. Steven Spielberg) and a few more

name actors, and Flockhart's TV-Q rating (a public-opinion poll that ranks celebrities in terms of likability and renown) was looking paltry by comparison. Didn't matter. Flockhart, again, stuck it out.

The play drew mixed reviews. Flockhart, personally, drew ecstatic reviews.

". . . Smashing," wrote the *New York Times'* Ben Brantley, in an otherwise cool notice.

Word like that gets around.

Back in Los Angeles, in the winter-spring of 1997, casting was under way for *Ally McBeal.*

"All along, we kept hearing about this Calista Flockhart, a theatrical actress in New York," *Ally* co-executive producer Jeffrey Kramer told Knight-Ridder News Service. "But we were told by people that she just wouldn't do television."

Around *Ally* offices, Flockhart was known as That Lady with the Name. After hundreds of would-be Allys read and failed to click, That Lady with the Name got another call. Flockhart was thoroughly New York–bound, thoroughly stagebound, but she took the call. And she read the script. As she told *Self,* it "touched" her.

David E. Kelley's words were enough to hook her. She flew to L.A. She auditioned. They liked. She left the room. Headed out of the studio. Got flagged down. Got informed the part was hers.

Then realized the gig meant she'd have to give up her place in New York.

"I don't know who I am [in Los Angeles]," she later told *USA Today.* "I'm driving with a cell phone hanging out of my ear, and I haven't driven in seven years!"

Flockhart never quite bargained that it would come to that—to that L.A. lifestyle. She's said she figured the worst (or best) that could come of *Ally* was that she'd shoot a few episodes, bank a few big paychecks and go home.

Figured wrong.

Ally was on its own timetable. *Ally* was its own monster. *Ally* devoured all—plans, free time, private lives.

Being Ally McBeal on an hourlong, weekly show named *Ally McBeal* meant seventeen-hour work days. Meant being on call for virtually every page, every scene.

When the show hit—and hit fast and big—being Ally McBeal also meant being Ally McBeal (or being viewed as such) every minute of every day. On the set and off.

Every interview became an exercise in, "So, how are you and Ally alike?" Every public appearance became a study of, "Look, she's moving her hands . . . *just like Ally*!" Every date, friendly or no, became fair target for paparazzi who wanted to document "Who's That New Man in Ally's Life?"

The stunned expression Flockhart wore when she won her *Ally* Golden Globe in January 1998—"She looks like she just got shot," an awards-night play-by-play report on E! Online noted—might as well have been a delayed reaction to the *Ally* phenomenon. Or a preemptive reaction to the *Ally* phenomenon to come.

In general, Flockhart played it cool. Yeah, she said, it's weird being suddenly famous, but it's okay. She claimed not to notice the unrelenting hype, the unrelenting press. If that was so, she missed some interesting stories. The one about how comic Garry Shandling picked her up at a TV critics awards dinner. The one about how she hiked up (and hiked up and . . .)

the hems on her already-short skirts. The one about how she was the "other" woman in the dissolving marriage between co-executive producer Jeffrey Kramer and his wife.

The one about how she was anorexic.

Absolutely no story dominated the beginning of Season No. 2 (not even that usual surefire attention-grabber, "Hey, it's Season No. 2!") more than the scuttlebutt about Flockhart, her weight—and reputed lack thereof.

To be sure, the *Ally* star was never considered wide-load material. She endured the occasional "skinny" gibe during the show's first year. You invite that sort of thing when you pretend to eat Ben & Jerry's onscreen before a nation of elastic-band-wearers who really eat Ben & Jerry's and know damn well what it makes them look like: *not* Calista Flockhart. Overall, though, the weight thing wasn't a big deal. Pundits were too busy debating whether she was taking an ax-sharp stiletto heel to the women's-rights movement to concern themselves with her dinner plans.

Unfortunately, the *Time* magazine cover sort of killed that fun. How do you top the sheer audacity, the sheer over-the-top madness of the news weekly's Susan B. Anthony vs. Ally stunt? You don't. You move on. And you wait . . . for something like the 1997–98 Primetime Emmy Awards.

There are fashion disasters—and then there are Fashion Chernobyls. Joan Rivers mops up the disasters, dishing and dissing them on the red carpet. (Christine Lahti not looking good tonight? Oh, well. . . . Next!) The Fashion Chernobyls can't be contained by Rivers. Or by a team of publicists. Or by modern science. The bad stuff just keeps leaking and leaking and leaking.

Calista Flockhart had a Fashion Chernobyl at the Emmys. She showed up at Los Angeles' Shrine Auditorium in a backless dress (here's betting, for the first and last time). Now, Flockhart apparently felt as if she had nothing to hide. But outsiders did. Tongues wagged. Onlookers reportedly gasped.

She was too thin!

From the Internet to the British tabs to the New York tabs, the word was the always-waifish Flockhart was becoming dangerously Karen Carpenteresque.

Then Season No. 2 started and Fox broadcast an episode featuring the size 2 Flockhart cavorting onscreen in a T-shirt and jeans. The actress apparently felt as if she had nothing to hide. But outsiders did.

She was too thin!

Flockhart and Fox finally responded with blanket denials: She's in the best shape of her life. Really.

On October 2, 1998, CBS's local news affiliate in New York City raised the hysteria stakes—erroneously reporting that production on *Ally* had been shut down. Shut down why? Because Flockhart supposedly had been admitted to the hospital for treatment of anorexia.

An hour later, the station broadcast a response from her publicist: No shutdown. No hospitalization. No problem. Calista's getting ready to "eat a bucket of chicken."

As if.

As if that was going to kill the rumors.

In subsequent days and weeks, Flockhart went Boris Yeltsin—going into heavy-duty damage-control mode to prove that everything was peachy-fine: showing up at a David E. Kelley tribute (in a back-*covered* dress, thank you very

much); firing an old publicist; hiring a new publicist; letting Fox "find" her in the stands at the World Series (while noshing on a bag of M&Ms, no less); issuing a statement of record on her height (5'5"), weight (102 pounds) and menu preferences (chicken, pasta or sushi for dinner, please!).

Must have been fun for a person already weirded out by people staring at her.

Must have been fun for a person already weary of being held up as a social model to be submitted as Exhibit A in the debate: *Do thin celebrities send unhealthy messages to young girls?*

Do they?

Did Roseanne—at her loudest and crassest and most zaftig—send *healthy* messages to young girls?

Did Jackie Gleason promote positive self-image for bus drivers?

Did Leonard Nimoy do justice to Vulcans?

No? Yes? Maybe?

Whatever.

You don't shut Chernobyl off with a switch. Nothing but time—lots of it—mitigates radioactive fallout.

As such, the Flockhart weight rumors—true, half-true or false—weren't going to be PRed away. Not until there was a new skinny person to obsess over, at least.

What was that about her sounding "battle weary"?

Just wait.

Calista Flockhart—Selected Credits

FILM

Like a Hole in the Head (upcoming)—Jill

A Midsummer Night's Dream (1999)—Helena
Telling Lies in America (1997)—Diney Majeski
Milk and Money (1997)—Christine
The Birdcage (1996)—Barbara Keeley
Drunks (1995)—Helen
Naked in New York (1994)
Quiz Show (1994)—Barnard Girl
Getting In (1994; short)—Amanda Morel
Clear Cut (1994; short)

TV

The Practice (ABC; guest star, 4/27/98)—Ally McBeal
Lifestories: Families in Crisis (HBO; guest star, 1992 episode,
    "The Secret Life of Mary-Margaret: Portrait of a
    Bulimic")—Mary-Margaret
Darrow (PBS; 1991; TV movie)—Lillian Anderson

STAGE

The Three Sisters (1997; Broadway)—Natalya Ivanovna
The Glass Menagerie (1994; Broadway)—Laura Wingfield
The Loop (1994; Off-Broadway)

COURTNEY THORNE-SMITH
(GEORGIA THOMAS)

Perhaps no *Ally* cast member was more equipped to deal with
The Whole *Ally* Thing (the media, the fans, the curious
Internet tradition wherein X-rated Webmeisters graft newly
famous heads onto pictures of anonymous nudes) than
Courtney Thorne-Smith.

Ally was The Whole *Melrose Place* Thing—Part II.

Thorne-Smith had lived through that. She could live through this.

She might even earn a little respect out of the whole deal.

"People speak to me as if I'm intelligent now," she told *People*.

Courtney Thorne-Smith was born just that: Courtney Thorne-Smith. The two-part last name isn't the result of some Chris Evert–turned–Chris Evert-Lloyd–turned–back-to–Chris Evert marriage/divorce mess. It's just the way her parents dubbed her on the birth certificate back on November 8, 1967. Thorne is her mother's maiden name. Smith is her father's surname.

"My mom was very forward-thinking," the Hyphenated One said in the *Buffalo News*.

Thorne-Smith and her sister, Jennifer, grew up in northern California, near San Francisco—a factoid that reassures us of our bearings. If a sunny California blonde (with a forward-thinking-hyphenated name) like Courtney Thorne-Smith *didn't* hail from California, then could we trust anything to be a slam-dunk?

Fortunately, everything was as it should have been: Thorne-Smith was a Californian. And, as of 1985, she was an actress—saved from a would-be academic career at Pennsylvania's Allegheny College by a talent scout who cast her in the sweet, geek-comes-of-age tale *Lucas*.

Thorne-Smith played Alise, the girlfriend of football jock Charlie Sheen. The movie also featured Corey Haim (who, with Corey Feldman, represented one half of the estimable 1980s film duo, The Two Coreys), Kerri Green and Winona Ryder, in her movie debut.

A decade later, Ryder was an A-list movie queen; Green, a pleasant Generation X–era footnote; and Haim and Sheen, screwups each worthy of an *E! True Hollywood Story* demitribute. And then there was Thorne-Smith—the one *Lucas* player who would have been easiest to dismiss, easiest to put down as an assembly-line ingenue—still around, still working—just like Ryder.

COURTNEY THORNE-SMITH IN FULL *MELROSE PLACE* HAIR PRIOR TO OPTING FOR A WORKING-WOMAN'S SPECIAL IN DEFERENCE TO HER NEW POSITION AS *ALLY* ASSOCIATE GEORGIA THOMAS.

© ALBERT L. ORTEGA/FLOWER CHILDREN LTD.

Unlike Ryder, Thorne-Smith's medium was to be television. Pin the blame (and credit) on the coloring. Pretty much since Jane Fonda lost her *Barbarella* blondeness and won an Oscar with her *Klute* look, the supposedly more serious school of film has been dominated by brunettes and Julia Roberts redheads. (Make no mistake: If Marilyn Monroe were starting her career today, her trademark platinum locks would be tinted Earthy Meryl Streep. Unless, of course, she intended to spend her career in *Naked Gun* sequels.)

TV, on the other hand, from Loni Anderson to Heather Locklear to Pamela Anderson, is built for blondes. It's the entertainment of the masses. And the masses (at least according to Madison Avenue) don't want to see egg-head women. They want *Babewatch*.

Which brings us back to Thorne-Smith. Her long, golden locks helped her land steady work in primetime at an age when her peers were struggling to pick majors in college. Her first regular series gig was, appropriately enough, the TV-ified version of a hit film: *Fast Times*, based on the 1982 comedy *Fast Times at Ridgemont High*. Thorne-Smith inherited the Jennifer Jason Leigh role of Stacy Hamilton, the sweet, sex-obsessed innocent. The show was on—and gone—in a month.

Film projects that played like glorified TV shows—minus the laugh tracks—followed; seminotably, *Summer School* with Mark Harmon, and *Revenge of the Nerds II: Nerds in Paradise* with Robert Carradine.

Then it was back to TV pretty much for good, starting with the 1988–89 NBC sitcom, *Day by Day*. Here, Thorne-Smith's tube persona was perfected: she was The Blonde Next Door. The guileless good girl who set off the hormones of teenage boys, oblivious to her considerable powers.

About the closest Thorne-Smith came to losing the goody-goody thing was in a guest stint in 1990 on the then all-powerful *L.A. Law*. There she was Kimberly, the bouncy, giggly Los Angeles Lakers cheerleader who dated no-fun Michael Kuzak (Harry Hamlin). Yes, it was yet another part built for a TV blonde. But there *was* a difference. This time, at least, her character was hardly guileless.

"When I showed up [for the] first day of work, there was a little tiny costume in my room," Thorne-Smith told the *Buffalo News*. "I said, 'Wait a minute!'"

Following *L.A. Law* she made one last real stab at features (1990's *Side Out*, a—what else?—beach-based volleyball

epic) before landing a leading part in the much-hyped *Beverly Hills 90210* spin-off—*Melrose Place*.

"I had heard about *Melrose Place* and didn't expect to like it," she told BPI Entertainment News Wire in 1992. "But I started reading and fell in love with Alison."

Alison was Alison Parker—the show's resident Blonde Next Door. (Actually, in its early, blander days, *MP* carried two Blondes Next Door, including Josie Bissett as Jane, the good doctor's wife. Given time and ratings pressures, both characters would drink, scheme and sleep around with the best of 'em. But that was given time.)

The show about twentysomethings started big, slumped and limped along—until Leading TV Blonde Heather Locklear sprang up in the spring of 1993 as man-stealin' barracuda Amanda Woodward. That did the trick. Once an earnest, if Aaron Spellingian attempt to depict lifestyles of the young and struggling, *MP* became *Dynasty* for a new generation. It also became a hit.

For a golden stretch from 1993 to 1995, *MP* ruled—if not in ratings (success on Fox is a relative thing, usually exclusive of the top ten), then everywhere else. It spawned posters, books, calendars, soundtracks and a devoted cult of fans. It made name actors of the previously uncelebrated (save for *Dynasty/T. J. Hooker* icon Locklear) cast.

In other words, it was *Ally*.

When *Ally* became *Ally*, Thorne-Smith was the obvious choice for other cast members to go to for advice on how to maneuver the business of starring on a hit show. She dispensed wisdom, she told *TV Guide*, on the ins and outs of photo shoots and awards shows. The good stuff.

But to get to *Ally*, Thorne-Smith first had to cut ties with *MP*. In a nice bit of timing, she exited the aging soap at the end of the 1996–97 season. Her once-indomitable heroine Alison was shipped off to . . . Atlanta. Something about her wanting to catch the Olympic spirit.

If that soapland snub wasn't bad enough (honestly, couldn't she have at least fallen into the *MP* pool—for a couple of dramatic *glub-glubs?*), Thorne-Smith had to endure a brief, if rare (for her) spell of unemployment. She was between gigs when the *Ally* pilot was shot in the spring of 1997—with actress Anna Gunn installed in the then-minor role of Georgia Thomas.

When the Georgia role became not-so-minor, Thorne-Smith got the call. If her still-flowing, California-dreamin' locks didn't exactly seem tailor-made for the part of a Boston lawyer, then she had other qualifications: like, she used to be Alison on *MP*, the show that was to be *Ally*'s time-slot companion.

During the course of the season, Thorne-Smith proved herself to be more than a mere ratings ploy to lure loyal *MP* fans. The Blonde Next Door held her own against a cast overwhelmingly made up of New York–tested stage actors. She proved capable of playing farce—even if her assignment, like that of TV husband Gil Bellows, was to perform the less flashy business of *reacting* to the madness around her.

Courtney Thorne-Smith—underneath all that hair, underneath all that *MP* baggage—was an actress. Who knew?

Back to the hair. There had to be a concession to her new, grown-up surroundings on *Ally*—and her hair was a good (the best?) place to start.

It had to be cut. It was cut. An end of an era—the beginning of a new one. This was the all-new Courtney Thorne-Smith. The one who appeared on Quasi-Important Television. The one who got good reviews from the *New York Times* even when she was slumming in a movie (*Chairman of the Board*) with—yeesh—Carrot Top in—double yeesh—her old hair. (An "admirable performance," the *Times'* Anita Gates opined.)

What a difference a TV season can make.

Contrasting *MP* and *Ally* for *People*, Thorne-Smith said: "The perception of the shows is so different. I used to get 'You're so pretty' from people when I was on *Melrose Place*.

"Now I get asked legal questions."

That, she could live through, too.

Courtney Thorne-Smith—Selected Credits

FILM

Chairman of the Board (1998)—Natalie
The Lovemaster (1996)—Deb
Side Out (1990)—Samantha
Revenge of the Nerds II: Nerds in Paradise (1987)—Sunny
Summer School (1987)—Pam
Lucas (1986)—Alise
Welcome to 18 (1986)—Lindsey

TV

Duckman (USA animated series; guest star, 2/8/97)—
    herself (voice)

Spin City (ABC; guest star, 1/14/97)—Danielle Brinkman
Breach of Conduct (USA; 1994; TV movie)—Helen Lutz
Melrose Place (Fox; series regular, 1992–97)—Alison Parker
Anything But Love (ABC; guest star, 1/17/90)—Allison
L.A. Law (NBC; recurring role, 1989–90 season)—Kimberly
Day by Day (NBC; series regular, 1988–89)—Kristin Carlson
Fast Times (CBS; series regular, 1986)—Stacy Hamilton

GREG GERMANN
(RICHARD FISH)

So, the guy tapped to play the series' resident attorney/shark starred on Broadway as a presidential assassin. . . . Damn typecasting.

Well, it was (kind of). In *Assassins*, a short-lived Stephen Sondheim musical (yes, musical), Germann handled the John Hinckley role. Now, if you had to assign rankings, Hinckley, the President Reagan gunman, would rate as one of the least financially and politically motivated of the murderous bunch. In short, hardly the stuff of a bottom-line Richard Fish.

Then again, Hinckley was about as certifiably daft as they come, too—so maybe *that* factor made Germann just the right guy to costar as a catchphrase-spouting cartoon on a certifiably daft TV series about lawyers.

Could be.

Nice thing about actors is, they just act—and leave the bone-digging to writers.

This is what Germann knows about *Ally McBeal*: "It's an amazing cast and amazing writing, and I end up looking forward to working."

He said that in the *Los Angeles Times*, in a mini-feature about how he spends his weekends. That anyone would care how Greg Germann, thespian–budding filmmaker (*Pete's Garden*)–budding playwright (*The Observatory*), spends his weekends (sometimes he and wife Christine Mourad listen to live mariachi music!) is further evidence yet of the power of *Ally*.

For the majority of his career, Germann was a working actor who did his job and went home at the end of the day (or night), unmolested by journalistic inquiries: *What's your favorite weekend like?*

Born in Houston, Germann started landing movie bits in his early twenties, in stuff like the unreleasable *The Whoopee Boys* (1986) with comic Paul Rodriguez. He eventually moved up in the film world, sharing screen time with proven box-office champs—like Chucky the Doll (*Child's Play 2*).

An apparent quest for sanity kept him based in New York, where Chucky the Doll was a two-bit piece of plastic and the roles were written by Neil Simon (*Biloxi Blues*).

In 1990, he landed the *Assassins* gig—and got to sing Sondheim (albeit in a production that sounded more like a *Simpsons* parody than an evening of grown-up theater). The show wasn't exactly long-running—or beloved. Like that mattered. You try passing up a chance to say you "sang" John Hinckley in a musical by the guy who wrote "Send in the Clowns." It doesn't really get much cooler than that.

After *Assassins*, Germann remained entrenched in New York, with occasional forays to Hollywood—the better to play Desk Clerk in a Mike Myers comedy (*So I Married an Axe Murderer*).

HOUSTON-BORN GREG
GERMANN NEVER INTENDED TO
MAKE HOLLYWOOD HIS HOME.
BUT THE TV JOBS—FROM *NED &
STACEY* TO *ALLY*—KEPT COMING.
© SUE SCHNEIDER/FLOWER CHILDREN LTD.

In 1994, he finally moved West for good—even if he didn't think so at the time.

"Before [my wife and I] came, I sort of had a little bit of a snobbery about television," he told *Viewers Voice*.

Sure, *before*. Snobbery as a concept is one thing, but you try passing up a full-on, full-paid, prime-time job. Germann didn't and couldn't. In the spring of 1994, he won a role in a new lawyer series. Unfortunately, it was a few years too early for *Ally McBeal*, so the series was called *Sweet Justice*. The stars were Melissa Gilbert (*Little House on the Prairie*) and Cicely Tyson (just about everything else). Germann played a scrapper of an eager-beaver law associate, name of Andy. He liked the part, liked the show. As if viewers—or network—cared. The series was canceled after one season.

That would have been the signal for Germann and wife to pack it in and head back East—except he got another series gig. This time, on a new Fox comedy, *Ned and Stacey*. Germann played the second-banana best married friend to couple-of-convenience Thomas Haden Church (late of *Wings*) and Debra Messing (future of *Will & Grace*). The network pushed and pushed and pushed and managed to eke out two low-rated seasons before pulling the plug in early 1997.

That would have been the signal to get out of town—except, again, there was a TV script to read. This time, the show was *Ally McBeal.* The part was Richard Fish.

"I knew it was an extremely well-written pilot—and I knew most of the other cast members from the theater in New York," Germann told E! Online. "So, with all that going for us, I was certain we were doomed."

Not this time.

Ally, obviously, clicked. Germann's "guileless" and "unapologetic" (his words) Fish clicked. All that, plus he got to work with Dyan Cannon—his finger to her wattle. "From Cary Grant to Burt Reynolds to Greg Germann," he told *Viewers Voice*, ticking off a list of Cannon's leading men. "She must be depressed."

Doubtful.

Greg Germann—Selected Credits

FILM

Pete's Garden (1998; short)—Pete (Also Writer-Director)
Clear and Present Danger (1994)—Petey
Imaginary Crimes (1994)—Mr. Drew
The Night We Never Met (1993)—Eddie
So I Married an Axe Murderer (1993)—Desk Clerk
Once Around (1991)—Jim Redstone
Child's Play 2 (1990)—Mattson
Miss Firecracker (1989)—Ronnie Wayne
The Whoopee Boys (1986)—Tipper

TV

Remember WENN (AMC; guest star, 8/14/98)—Arden Sage

Ned and Stacey (Fox; series regular, 1995–97)—Eric Moyer

Ellen (ABC; guest star, three episodes starting 3/30/94)—
 Rick

Sweet Justice (NBC; series regular, 1994–95)—Andy Del
 Sarto

Assault at West Point: The Court-Martial of Johnson Whittaker
 (Showtime; 1994; TV movie)—Bailey

Tour of Duty (CBS; guest star, three episodes during
 1989–90 season)—Lieutenant Beller

Taking the Heat (Showtime; 1993; TV movie)—Kennedy

STAGE

Assassins (1990; Broadway)—John Hinckley

MUSIC

Broadway cast album:

Assassins (1991; RCA/Victor)

LISA NICOLE CARSON
(RENEE RADICK)

If you had to pick the one *Ally* cast member most likely to supply the quote, "I take no shit from anyone," Calista Flockhart would come in a disappointing last. The resident nice guys (Bellows, Germann, MacNicol) would come in a close (and joint) next-to-last.

This would leave three probable suspects: Courtney Thorne-Smith, Jane Krakowski and Lisa Nicole Carson.

Thorne-Smith? Nah. On one hand, the line does sound as if it could have been featured in an R-rated *Melrose Place*. On the other hand, it's an Amanda line, not an Alison line.

Krakowski? Maybe. The quote's brassy. It's showy. It just doesn't feel Broadway—Krakowski's second home. If the collective plays of David Mamet have taught us anything, it's that the cuss word of choice among stage folk begins with an *f*. (There's just something about how that clipped "-uck" sound carries to the back row.)

Carson? Yup.

Why?

She just seems kind of feisty that way.

Or, then again, maybe that reasoning is the product of the "oh, she's just like the character on her show" syndrome.

But what are you going to do when Carson says she *is* a bit like her headstrong, sense-talking, suffer-no-fools TV self?

"I'm pretty bold and for the most part we're alike," Carson said in *Black Elegance*—a couple sentences after issuing the "take no shit" position.

Well, it's unanimous, then. Cool person Renee Radick is portrayed by cool person Lisa Nicole Carson.

To a point.

Apparently not thinking it'd be in her best interest to have the collective TV nation thinking she could (and would) drop-kick them like kung fu–fighting Renee, Carson likes to say her alter ego is a tad too intense for her taste. Carson is, after all, a woman who has let it be known early and often that she's a free spirit—she literally wears a "Gypsy" tattoo (among others).

JUST SO YOU DON'T MISS THE POINT, PERFORMER'S-PERFORMER LISA NICOLE CARSON WEARS A 'GYPSY' TATTOO ON HER ARM.
© ALBERT L. ORTEGA/FLOWER CHILDREN LTD.

"My friends can't believe I'm playing the cool, calm and collected one," she once told *People*.

Of course, on *Ally*, "cool, calm and collected" is a relative thing.

Carson was born on July 12, 1969 (under the sign of Cancer, the crab—the inspiration for the second of her three tattoos), in Brooklyn, New York. This daughter of teachers always had her ambitions set on the spotlight. At age eight, she was nailing it in a school production of *Fiddler on the Roof*. She played Yente, the middle-aged Jewish matchmaker at the social center of an early-1900s Russian village. She was *eight*.

When she was about twenty-two, she was no less ambitious. If she wasn't singing on *The Apollo Comedy Hour*, where she was a featured performer, she was landing acting gigs on primetime shows like *Law & Order* and *The Cosby Show*.

The *Cosby* assignment was one of those big-break opportunities that didn't quite break. She told *USA Weekend* that she was supposed to have two lines on the long-running sitcom's much-hyped 1992 series finale. *Was supposed to have.* The lines got cut. Carson was left making like a silent-film actor, hoping her extra-emotive facial expressions would sell her noncharacter, would tell the TV audience: "I had lines to say, and if you could hear them, they'd be damn good!" she said in the weekly.

In the end, the *Cosby* farewell itself was overshadowed by the Los Angeles riots—Carson just wasn't fated to pull a win out of that one.

No matter. The feisty move on—to the next (not quite) big-break opportunity.

Divas (1995) was supposed to be a series for ABC about a girl singing group—a chance for Carson to showcase her pipes as well as her acting. *Was supposed to be.* Despite the backing of TV creative heavyweight Thomas Carter (*Equal Justice, Don King: Only in America*), the project never got past the pilot stage.

No matter. She was still moving on. Later that year, she scored a nifty, seductive turn in Denzel Washington's *Devil in a Blue Dress*. In 1996, she landed a recurring role on TV's top-rated show, playing *ER* doctor Eriq LaSalle's sometime girlfriend and mother of his child.

Then—finally—the big break. The real one. *Ally* co-executive producer Jeffrey Kramer remembered Carson from *Divas* (maybe that project wasn't so doomed, after all) and suggested her for the role of prosecutor Renee Radick. Bingo.

She spent most of the first season on her own little *Ally* subseries. More than being the show's only black regular (and sometimes it's only black performer, period), she was the only character not tied to Fish/Cage. (Well, unless you count Vonda—but she sings during the entire blinkin' show, so it's not like her absence is exactly profound.) Carson was called on to keep Flockhart's Ally company in the home-front scenes. Apparently Kelley figured (rightly) that if he didn't

keep somebody around to yell at his flaky heroine every week, bricks might start flying in the direction of TV sets. Carson made the most of her least opportunities. When the show let her rip—notably in Renee's inexplicable nightclub singing scenes—she let it rip. All this, while keeping up with her *ER* gig and whatever else came along. One night in April 1998, she appeared in every show on Fox's Monday night lineup, which in addition to *Ally*, meant guest stints on its two lead-in sitcoms, *Damon* and *Getting Personal*.

The off-season was no less packed: making a movie with Eddie Murphy (*Life*), working her music career, singing the National Anthem at the World Series.

Success was tiring, but not bullying, to Carson.

She doesn't take any you-know-what and she's got a third tattoo: a drawing of two fists breaking chains.

Lisa Nicole Carson—Selected Credits

FILM

Life (upcoming)
Eve's Bayou (1997)—Matty Mereaux
Love Jones (1997)—Josie Nichols
Devil in a Blue Dress (1995)—Coretta James
Jason's Lyric (1994)—Marti

TV

Damon (Fox; guest star, 4/27/98)—Lieutenant Byrne
Getting Personal (Fox; guest star, 4/27/98)
ER (NBC; recurring role, 1996–)—Carla Reese
Divas (ABC; TV movie; 1995)—Jewel

The Cosby Show (NBC; non-speaking role, 4/30/92)
Law & Order (NBC; guest star, 10/1/91)—Jasmine

JANE KRAKOWSKI
(ELAINE VASSAL)

The first thing you notice about Jane Krakowski are the eyes. To call them big would make it sound like they're buggy—which they're not. To call them Bette Davis–like would conjure unneeded memories of schmaltzy 1980s pop hits. To call them arresting just might do it.

To say that it's borderline disturbing to see said eyes (and head) inflated like a Macy's Thanksgiving Day balloon by the post-production whizzes at *Ally* is an understatement.

"It's *not* my favorite special effect that they're using at this moment," Krakowski deadpanned to *Soap Opera News*.

No, but such are the indignities one must endure for the sake of a gimme, gimmick laugh. Not to mention, for the shot at breakout stardom.

It's too soon to tell if the thing that Krakowski is achieving on *Ally* is genuine Hollywood stardom (i.e., something that'll lead to regular, big-time movie work, or at least her own series) or if it's a high-profile respite from a stage career. Her character, the TV law firm's busybody assistant, Elaine Vassal, isn't necessarily one that lends itself to long-term viability. Rather, it's one of those quirky, larger-than-life roles that delivers the equivalent of a sugar rush to the audience— Elaine Vassal, as quick-fix, quick-hit entertainment: "Oh, look, that Elaine! She's funny!" Replace the name "Elaine" with the name of any quirky, larger-than-life character from a

JANE KRAKOWSKI SAYS SHE
CALLED ON THE POWERS OF THE
WONDERBRA TO HELP ACE HER
ALLY AUDITION FOR BUSY-BODY
SECRETARY ELAINE VASSAL.
© ALBERT L. ORTEGA/FLOWER CHILDREN LTD.

once-beloved show like *Northern Exposure*, *Twin Peaks* or *L.A. Law*—and you get the idea. To save their lives, most people today wouldn't be able to come up with a name—any name—for one of those quirky, larger-than-life characters. That young guy from *Northern Exposure*—whatzhis-name?—the one who was really smart, but kind of weird and shy . . . ? Time's up. (*Answer:* Ed. Played by Darren E. Burrows.)

All of this, of course, is probably a moot point to Krakowski. She's been working on Broadway since she was eighteen—and the theater community will probably have her until she's eighty-eight. Talent will out. Except in Hollywood, where talent—like standards—is negotiable.

Krakowski does not hail from Hollywood, nor the West Coast. She was born in 1969 in Broadway-accessible Parsippany, New Jersey. The family surname was Krajkowski—the spare *j* ditched to make the lives of casting directors forever easier.

"She started dancing at three," her mother, Barbara Krajkowski, a college theater teacher, said in William Paterson University's online newsletter, *Cybernews*. "She was always interested in art and we always knew she had stage talent."

Directors knew she had stage talent, too. As a kid, she won parts in community theater and the occasional commer-

cial. As a newly minted teenager, she snagged screen time in the 1983 Chevy Chase comedy, *National Lampoon's Vacation*. She played Cousin Vicki—the kid with the line about how she knows she's really good at French kissing . . . because her father tells her so. (Rim shot, please!) Well, it was what it was—a little piece of cult-movie infamy at age fourteen.

At fifteen, she won a contract role in the now-defunct NBC soap *Search for Tomorrow*. From 1984 to 1986, Krakowski served the perfunctory function of Daytime Drama Troubled Teen. Her performance as T. R. Kendall was lauded with two Daytime Emmy nominations.

The hit parade continued. At age eighteen, she was roller-skating—as part of Broadway's mechanized Andrew Lloyd Webber musical *Starlight Express*. In 1990, she was getting the spotlight in Tommy Tune's majestic *Grand Hotel*. Krakowski played a typist whose bottle-blonde hair gave her the air of the movie star she dreamed of becoming. One of her songs: "I Want to Go to Hollywood."

The role earned Krakowski a Tony nomination, but her own Hollywood career was as fitful as that of *Grand Hotel*'s Flaemmchen. There was work here (*Stepping Out*, with Liza Minnelli in 1991) and there was work there (a bit in *Fatal Attraction* in 1987), but nothing substantial. TV and film knows what to do with a Demi Moore type. It doesn't know what to do with a Jane Krakowski type, especially in an actress' starlet years. Employability that can't be explained with *Playboy* Bunny terms (36–24–36) gets overlooked.

With her brassy belting ability, Krakowski found it more difficult to be overlooked on Broadway. In between her sporadic Hollywood forays in the 1990s, she moved from one big

New York stage show to another: *Company*, with Tony-winner Boyd Gaines; the play *Tartuffe: Born Again*; and *Once Upon a Mattress* with Sarah Jessica Parker.

In spring 1997, she got a new nibble from the West Coast. A chance to read for a new David E. Kelley series for Fox. En route to her final *Ally* audition, she bumped into fellow New York stage actress Calista Flockhart, also a finalist in the series' late casting round. Krakowski and Flockhart went way back—Krakowski's best friend was Flockhart's roommate at Rutgers University. Krakowski told *People* that the two bolstered each other during their nervous countdown time—talking on the plane, hanging in their Los Angeles hotel, wishing each other luck the next morning.

While Flockhart later expressed ambivalence about doing a TV series, Krakowski was ready for the gig. If anybody was going to be the potentially grating Elaine Vassal, she wanted it to be her. Her audition getup: "The tightest sweater that I own, with a Wonderbra," she recalled in *People*.

Clearly this was a woman in sync with a character who later, as prompted by Kelley's script, would come to hawk something called a "face bra."

"When Jane enters a room, she *enters* a room, and when she leaves a room, she's *still* in the room," Kelley said in *TV Guide*.

In other words, Kelley had found his Elaine; Krakowski had found her Hollywood niche.

Krakowski wasn't sure if the new gig would last—TV's infant-mortality rate being the highest among the globe's civilized communities (or, in TV's case, *mostly* civilized)—but she wasn't about to pass it up. No actor's ever dead-set sure

which project will work, which won't. You get the best script, best deal, best chance you can—and hope for the best.

Krakowski and company escaped from *Ally*'s Season No. 1 unscathed. So far, so good. They're ahead of the game.

The show's hit status is more than Krakowski could have banked on—that also goes for the new record deal and the upcoming movie *Go*, with Taye Diggs (*How Stella Got Her Groove Back*) and Katie Holmes (*Dawson's Creek*).

So, this is what it was: Sometimes the impossible *can* be done. The actress with *those eyes* and that theater-bound career was making her very own Nick at Nite moments, becoming as much a part of the primetime universe as the Olsen twins or Don Johnson.

Such are the indignities one must endure for glory.

Jane Krakowski—Selected Credits

FILM

Go (upcoming)—Irene
Dance with Me (1998)—Patricia
Mrs. Winterbourne (1996)—Christine
Stepping Out (1991)—Lynne
Fatal Attraction (1987)—Babysitter
Vacation (1983)—Cousin Vicki

TV

Due South (CBS; guest star, 4/6/96)—Katherine Burns
Alex Haley's 'Queen' (ABC; TV miniseries; 1993)—Jane
Search for Tomorrow (NBC; series regular, 1984–86)—
   Rebecca "T. R." Kendall

STAGE

Once Upon a Mattress (Broadway; 1996)—Lady Larken
Tartuffe: Born Again (Broadway; 1996)—Maryann
Company (Broadway; 1995)—April
Grand Hotel (Broadway; 1991)—Flaemmchen, the Typist
Starlight Express (Broadway)

MUSIC
Compilations:
The Burt Bacharach Album (1998; UNI/Varese Sarabande)—
    Krakowski track: "The Look of Love"
Lost in Boston IV (1997; UNI/Varese Sarabande)—
    Krakowski track (duet with Sal Viviano): "I'm Naïve"
Sondheim at the Movies (1997; UNI/Varese Sarabande)—
    Krakowski track: "Sooner or Later"

Broadway cast albums:
Once Upon a Mattress (1997; RCA Victor)
Company (1996; Angel)
Grand Hotel (1992; BMG Classics)

PETER MACNICOL
(JOHN CAGE)

Peter MacNicol once described his *Ally* character, John Cage, as a "mooncalf."

What the *hell* is a mooncalf, you ask?

Not important. (It's a seventeenth-century term for a foolish person.) The important thing is *MacNicol* knows what the hell a "mooncalf" is.

No, the role of law-firm partner John Cage should not be left to the devices of an actor with a puny vocabulary. You need to know *lots* of words when you play John Cage. You need to *read* lots of books when you play John Cage. Otherwise, you might get too locked in to a script—with nothing to stare or think about *but* John Cage. No good can come of such a thing.

PETER MACNICOL HAS DESCRIBED HIS *ALLY* CHARACTER AS A 'MOONCALF,' ONE OF THE NICER TERMS FOR THE MADDENING JOHN CAGE.
© ALBERT L. ORTEGA/FLOWER CHILDREN LTD.

Because John Cage *is* a mooncalf.

And, to a degree, Peter MacNicol has no one to blame but himself.

Take the first *Ally* episode in which MacNicol appeared, Season No. 1's "Compromising Positions." At the time, it was to be the *only Ally* episode in which MacNicol appeared.

David E. Kelley envisioned John Cage as a one-trick, one-episode pony—the slick, moneyed guy who swoops in and tries to explain away a prostitution rap.

Problem was, Kelley gave MacNicol the script. Asked him to play Cage. Asked him, in one particular scene, to pour a glass of water.

Trouble.

Somebody didn't do a scouting report on MacNicol. Somebody missed the 1982 *New York Times* profile on MacNicol. The one headlined: "He Gets Wrapped Up in Other People's Lives."

Okay, so that water-pouring scene? It was no big deal. At least the way it was described in the script. But MacNicol seized the opportunity to make a big impression.

"I said, 'I am not going to simply pour a glass of water,'" MacNicol told *TV Guide*. "'I am going to pour the longest glass of water in television history, for the sheer shock value of it.'"

And thus the mooncalf was birthed—on its (his?) way to becoming, arguably, the most popular *Ally* player behind Calista Flockhart and Vonda Shepard. By episode six, he had secured his place as a regular cast member.

If all continues swimmingly, MacNicol's hit-show exposure may help clear up a couple of long-standing misconceptions: (1) that he's the brother of former child star Kristy (*Family*) McNichol; and (2) that he starred in *Porky's*.

"I swear to God, I think my mother feels I was in it," he said of the 1981 peephole comedy, in an online chat on *Talk City*.

(Note to Mother MacNicol: Not to disappoint, but that's Dan Monahan, as Pee Wee, whom you're probably confusing for Sonny there.)

The *real* Peter MacNicol was born April 10, 1954, in Dallas, Texas. The *real* Peter MacNicol grew up in both the Lone Star state and Minnesota, forever searching for the *real* Peter MacNicol. As a kid, he fancied searching for fossils in the Gobi Desert. As a college student, he pursued theater— even if he was unconvinced that acting was what the *real* Peter MacNicol was meant to do. At one point, the world of Franciscan monks looked like an employment option.

Certainly, others were convinced that acting was MacNicol's profession. He worked in repertory theater at

Minnesota's Guthrie Theater for two years in the late 1970s. In 1981, at age twenty-seven, he starred on Broadway in Beth Henley's Southern-fried sister-act play, *Crimes of the Heart*, with Holly Hunter.

In the movies that same year, he starred in the dreary sword-and-sorcery drama, *Dragonslayer*. What looked like a career breakthrough was almost a career-breaker. MacNicol did not have a pleasant time in chain mail. He did not have a pleasant time pretending to slay make-believe dragons. He was, after all, Peter MacNicol, not Arnold Schwarzenegger. As Leonard Maltin's film guide delicately put it, he was "somewhat incongruously" cast.

MacNicol—how should we say?—freaked. He told the *New York Times* that he felt he'd betrayed his art. Nagging doubts returned. MacNicol fled.

"I was traveling like some sort of pilgrim in search of an urging," he told the *Times*, in that long-ago 1982 profile. "I didn't know what I was going to do."

While fishing in Minnesota, he got an inkling—and returned to New York for a new movie audition.

The audition (which MacNicol aced) was for That One Great Credit—the one that nobody gets to take away, no matter how bad you stink or screwup from that time hence.

The movie was *Sophie's Choice*, the post–World War II drama about one woman's awful Holocaust memories. MacNicol was Stingo, the wide-eyed, virtual stand-in for author William Styron (on whose novel the film was based). Sophie was Oscar-winner Meryl Streep and her Oscar-winning Polish accent. Kevin Kline played her lover, Nathan.

The film was released in December 1982—primed for the award season. Critics lost it over Streep, lost it over Kline, lost it over the cinematography. MacNicol got strong notices, too, but, ultimately, he got plain lost. And when some critics went looking for reasons why *Sophie's Choice*, the film, didn't quite match Streep, the performance, in the revelatory department, Stingo got stung. He was perceived as the quiet guy slowing down the works.

When it was time to distribute the shiny-gift hardware, MacNicol came up empty.

And when it came time to pick a follow-up role, Streep went the way of *The French Lieutenant's Woman*. Kline began work on *The Big Chill*.

MacNicol did a play in New Haven, Connecticut.

The move was his choice. He didn't run after Hollywood. Hollywood didn't run after him. He was, like Stingo, "off to the side of things," as he said in the *Times*.

MacNicol kept to the stage through most of the rest of the 1980s, if starring in Broadway productions of Shakespeare can be called being "kept." In 1986, he played groom in his wedding to Marsue Cumming. And in 1987, he finally scored his next notable feature role as the wild-haired Janosz Poha in *Ghostbusters II*, otherwise known as the anti–*Sophie's Choice*.

He became comfortable enough with acting in 1992 to accept the closest thing in the modern-day thespian craft to a Joe Lunchpail job: a network sitcom. The show was *The Powers That Be*, a Norman Lear–produced NBC series about a dopey United States senator. John Forsythe was the dopey senator; MacNicol, in the David Hyde Pierce role, was the

preppy press secretary. (Pierce, he of preppy *Frasier* fame, was unavailable—seeing as how he had *another* part in the series.) MacNicol didn't have a chance to become disillusioned with the sitcom form. *The Powers That Be* quickly became so much primetime roadkill.

MacNicol was back to doing occasional film work (notably, 1993's *Addams Family Values*, and unnotably, 1995's *Dracula: Dead and Loving It*) when David E. Kelley decided he needed a lawyer.

It was 1994 and Kelley was launching his new CBS medical drama, *Chicago Hope*. A hospital full of doctors and nurses apparently made the attorney in Kelley nervous. He wanted a legal guy around—and created the role of hospital advocate Alan Birch, otherwise known as "the Eel," not to be confused with "the Biscuit," the nickname of the *other* Kelley lawyer MacNicol would come to play.

Seeing as how *Chicago Hope* was about medicine and *not* law, the Eel did not have the showy opportunities that the Biscuit would. MacNicol felt buried in the cast. When Kelley abdicated the day-to-day writing chores on the series at the end of the first season, MacNicol's chances got even slimmer. He asked off the show. He was granted his wish. By the fall of 1995, his character was dead meat. (It would take a ghost appearance in the fall of 1998 to stage MacNicol's—brief—return.)

Frustrating but useful was how MacNicol looked on the *Chicago Hope* experience.

Once he let go of feeling slighted, he said on *Talk City*, he remembered that he was "acting to act and not acting for fame."

Thanks to the little glass-pouring stunt on *Ally* in 1997, MacNicol finally found both—a good role, a tidy level of fame.

For better, or arguably for worse, the oddball antics of Cage came to dominate the tone of Kelley's already off-kilter series. What started out as a show about one off-center young woman, under the regular influence of MacNicol's Cage, became a show about a circusful of geeks. ("Step inside, folks! Step inside! Nose-whistling like you've never heard! Shoe-squeaking that'll make you squeal! Moment-taking that'll leave you breathless! . . . Did we mention bagpipes?")

"I'm a patsy for his work," Kelley told *USA Today*, under-scoring the obvious.

The mooncalf won.

Peter MacNicol—Selected Credits

FILM
Bean (1997)—David Langley
Toto Lost in New York (1996)—Ork (voice only)
Dracula: Dead and Loving It (1995)—Renfield
Radioland Murders (1994)—Son Writer
Addams Family Values (1993)—Gary Granger
HouseSitter (1992)—Marty
Hard Promises (1991)—Stuart
American Blue Note (1989)—Jack Solow
Ghostbusters II (1989)—Janosz Poha
Heat (1987)—Cyrus Kinnick
Sophie's Choice (1982)—Stingo
Dragonslayer (1981)—Galen

TV

Chicago Hope (CBS; guest star, 10/29/98)—Alan Birch

Silencing Mary (NBC; 1998; TV movie)—Lawrence Dixon

Abducted: A Father's Love (NBC; 1996; TV movie)—Roy
    Dowd

Chicago Hope (CBS; series regular, 1994–95)—Alan Birch

Roswell (Showtime; 1994; TV movie)—Lewis Rickett

Cheers (NBC; guest star, 4/1/93)—Mario

The Powers That Be (NBC; 1992–93)—Bradley Grist

By Dawn's Early Light (HBO; 1990)—Sedgewicke

STAGE

Black Comedy/White Liars (1993; Broadway)—Brindsley
    Miller/Frank

Romeo and Juliet (1988; New York Shakespeare Festival)—
    Romeo

The Nerd (1987; Broadway)—Rick Steadman

Richard II (1987; New York Shakespeare Festival)—
    Richard II

Crimes of the Heart (1981; Broadway)—Barnette Lloyd

GIL BELLOWS
(BILLY THOMAS)

Gil Bellows once told *USA Today* that the longest he'd lasted
in a job prior to *Ally McBeal* was five months. That was it.
Five months. It's not as aimless as it sounds. You don't go into
acting to punch a time clock and fill out a break card. But a
little security every now and then? The notion had its appeal.
If a hit series meant security, then so be it—bring it on. A

married man and fresh inductee into the class of thirtysomethings, Gil Bellows, in 1997, was ready to embrace something as crazy and grueling as a weekly TV show.

Bellows came to *Ally* with a batch of solid credits, but nothing that put him over the top or made him instantly recognizable at the length of a red carpet. Prior to the show's premiere, he was best known as the guy who kind of looked like Matthew Broderick (but wasn't) in the film (*Miami Rhapsody*) that kind of sounded like it was written by Woody Allen (but wasn't). Or, as the guy who got the part (Tommy Williams) that reputedly was reserved for Brad Pitt (but wasn't) in the film (*The Shawshank Redemption*) that got nominated for a bunch of Oscars.

Ally would end the confusion—make Gil Bellows simply Gil Bellows—even if David E. Kelley did hand him the show's blandest role and, in turn, toughest assignment. With attorney Billy Thomas, Bellows was asked to play the series' Hamletesque second lead—the nice guy who was just slightly indecisive enough about his intentions toward his wife, Georgia, and his first love, Ms. McBeal, to keep him from blending (completely) with the paneling. If America would learn soon enough Billy was a drip, Bellows wasn't complaining.

"I'm glad for the situation I'm in in my life . . ." he said in *TV Guide*.

Here's how he got here from there: Born in Vancouver, Canada, Bellows migrated south to do the thespian thing at the Pasadena, California, home of the American Academy of Dramatic Arts—proving ground for marquee names like Robert Redford and Danny DeVito. Stage work (mostly on

the other, Eastern coast) followed: roles in plays from *King Lear* to *Diary of Anne Frank.* The stage was good to Bellows—professionally, personally. In 1991, at the Williamstown Theater Festival in Massachusetts, he met future wife Rya Kihlstedt. Kihlstedt was an actress, too. (She'd go on to grab some marquee space of her own in 1997's fizzled, one-sequel-too-far comedy, *Home Alone 3.*) On Valentine's Day 1994, Bellows proposed; Kihlstedt accepted. If you must know—and Bellows either (*a*) wanted you to know, or (*b*) didn't fully grasp he was sharing this tidbit with a national publication, he and Kihlstedt, as he told *TV Guide*, sealed their engagement with "passionate sex." (As always, thanks for sharing.)

PLEASANTLY HANDSOME GIL BELLOWS PLAYS BLANDLY PLEASANT BILLY THOMAS ON *ALLY*—AN EXAMPLE OF A PERFECT MARRIAGE BETWEEN ACTOR AND CHARACTER.
© ALBERT L. ORTEGA/FLOWER CHILDREN LTD.

The love-life thing sorted out (and, no, he told interviewers, he didn't have a real-life Ally complex over a past love—as if he'd ever spill *that one* to a reporter), Bellows career started to sort itself out, too. There were a couple of primetime guest shots (including one, in a tidy bit of career synchronicity, on NBC legal-eagle series *Law & Order*) and a couple of big-screen, big-time movie gigs, chiefly *The Shawshank Redemption* (1994).

Based on a Stephen King novella, *The Shawshank Redemption* was, in the hang-'em-high 1990s, a quaint throw-

back—a defendant's movie, wherein the good guys were behind bars and the bad guys were the jailers. Tim Robbins and Morgan Freeman starred as the noblest of the noble prisoners. Bellows found himself at the mess table with the big boys as innocent-looking inmate Tommy Williams. The role was said to have been floated the way of golden boy Brad Pitt. But it was fated to go Bellows' way. If ever there was an actor uniquely qualified to play a Tommy or a Billy or some equally benign-sounding character, it was Bellows and his unthreatening, senior-class-president handsomeness.

The critical success of *Shawshank* meant Bellows got more film work, but it didn't make him a name-brand actor. More perplexing, neither did his first romantic quasi-lead. *Miami Rhapsody* was a 1995 comedy about love and commitment (or lack thereof) starring Sarah Jessica Parker and written and directed by David Frankel (channeling Woody Allen, right down to the Mia Farrow hire). Bellows played Matt, Parker's benign (natch) boyfriend who wanted to get married. The two made for a cute onscreen couple—if partly because Bellows, holding down the film's Matthew Broderick role, looked a lot like a taller version of Parker's offscreen partner, one Matthew Broderick. Not surprisingly, *Miami Rhapsody*, a dud at the box office, didn't do a whole lot to raise Bellows' profile. It was the kind of movie where critic Roger Ebert could write a positive, three-star review and make but one reference to Bellows (in parentheses, no less).

Mild-mannered Billy Thomas was Bellows' savior; the role that rescued him from independent movies featuring Justine (*Family Ties*) Bateman. (The two costarred in a little-seen flick called *The Assistant*.) Bellows landed the *Ally* gig in

early 1997 and the next thing you know he's making a film with Emma Thompson (*Judas Kiss*).

Billy also proved a friend in protecting Bellows from the *Ally* media crush. When the show hit, Billy wasn't the character that got the buzz buzzing. Billy was *nice*—he wasn't a guy with a remote-control toilet flusher (i.e., Peter MacNicol's John Cage), he wasn't a guy with cute catchphrases (i.e., Greg Germann's Richard Fish), he wasn't a nightclub singer (i.e., Vonda Shepard), he wasn't a woman with a dream about a face bra (i.e., Jane Krakowski's Elaine Vassal) and he wasn't a leggy blonde in a wraparound washcloth (Calista Flockhart's Ally). In the insane TV year of 1997–98, Bellows found himself on a sane little island. He had success. He had a manageable degree of acclaim. He had his own life. No one was putting his face on *Time* magazine, linking Billy Thomas to famous dull guys throughout history.

It was good to be Gil Bellows.

Gil Bellows—Selected Credits

FILM

Dinner at Fred's (upcoming)—Richard
Judas Kiss (1999)—Lizard Browning
Snow White: A Tale of Terror (1997)—Will
Looking for Richard (1996)
The Substance of Fire (1996)—Val Chenard
Miami Rhapsody (1995)—Matt
Black Day Blue Night (1995)—Hitchhiker Dodge
Silver Strand (1995)—Brian Del Piso
Love and a .45 (1994)—Watty Watts

The Shawshank Redemption (1994)—Tommy Williams

TV
The Practice (ABC; guest star, 4/27/98)—Billy Thomas
Radiant City (CBS; 1996; TV movie)—Bert Kramer
Flying Blind (Fox; guest star, 10/4/92)—Gerard
Law & Order (NBC; guest star, 2/5/91)—Howard Metzler

VONDA SHEPARD
(THE SINGER)

It's proper journalistic style to refer to a person, upon second reference, by his or her last name. But the rules don't work with Vonda Shepard. To call Vonda anything but Vonda, somehow seems to miss the point entirely.

Vonda Shepard is not about the "proper" way to do things. She's not about the "rules." She's about being a singer-songwriter who kicked around for two decades before finally finding album and touring fame through a hit primetime TV show about lawyers.

The next performer who turns that trick will be the second.

Born in New York City circa 1963, Shepard was the product of an appropriately electric environment. (Translation: Her father was a mime—as well as an actor and a director. Her mother was a model.) She was raised in southern California. (Looking for a Maryland connection? There is none. The main source for the *Ally* soundtrack song "Maryland," she has said, is pretty much her imagination. She never lived there, never left there. Although, she told the *Washington Post*, her mother *did* talk about moving there.)

The kid who used to "rock the crib and sing out loud all night long," as she noted in an America Online chat, grabbed a keyboard and crashed the music business at age fourteen—playing local Los Angeles clubs at the tail end of the touchy-feely singer-songwriter 1970s.

FROM BACK-UP GIGS TO CHART-TOPPING SOLO SUCCESS: VONDA SHEPARD'S HORATIO ALGER TALE WOULD HAVE BEEN PERFECT IF HER RISE HADN'T BEEN TIED TO THE SOULLESS 'SEARCHIN' MY SOUL.'
© SUE SCHNEIDER/FLOWER CHILDREN LTD.

By her early twenties, she was touring as a backup vocalist and keyboardist for Al Jarreau (a TV crooner himself, with 1985's *Moonlighting* theme) and touchy-feely singer-songwriter icons Jackson Browne ("Runnin' on Empty") and Rickie Lee Jones ("Chuck E.'s in Love").

The Rickie Lee Jones connection seems particularly apt. If you were forced to describe Vonda Shepard to a Martian (a Martian with a working knowledge of modern-day American pop music), you could do worse than say she's like a lesser Rickie Lee Jones with Carly Simon's mouth and Sheryl Crow's clothes. You could do better, too. You could avoid an argument and delete the "lesser" reference. You could say, Vonda Shepard's really great and lots of people really seem to like her music. You *could* say that. But you're not that savvy. So you stick with the "lesser" reference and hope people will take it in the spirit of criticism—and decide not to hurt you. (Much.)

In any case, Vonda's got bigger fish to fry than you, the person trying to describe her music to a Martian. This was a

woman who bravely and gamely tried to launch a Rickie Lee Jones–type solo career in the mid-1980s. Know this: Even *Rickie Lee Jones* couldn't launch a Rickie Lee Jones solo career in the mid-1980s. The mid-1980s were the age of hair bands and synthesizers and Early Madonna (The Boy-Toy Years). There was little room for earthy chicks who fashioned themselves earnest, piano-playing singer-songwriters.

She found a tiny bit of air in 1987. She recorded a duet with Dan Hill (he, of the *ultra*touchy-feely 1970s hit, "Sometimes When We Touch"). The track, "Can't We Try," became a Top Ten single. In short time, she signed her own solo deal with Reprise Records.

The above proves what more than a little perseverance can produce; i.e., you *can* wear down the marketplace. But the following proves that perseverance can only produce so much; i.e., given the chance, the marketplace can—and will—wear *you* down.

Sure, Vonda had a record deal. And, sure, Vonda had an album, a 1989 self-titled disc. But did Vonda have any hit singles? Radio airplay? *Tonight Show* gigs? Major concert tours?

Nope. The album tanked. So did its 1992 follow-up, *The Radical Light*, featuring not only the future theme of *Ally McBeal* ("Searchin' My Soul") but the future title of one of its episodes ("100 Tears Away"). Unfortunately, *Ally* didn't exist back then. Record-buyers ignored the release. Reprise cut Vonda loose.

Funny thing about success is, the difference between Vonda the perceived failure of 1992, and Vonda the celebrated success of 1998, is not that great. "Searchin' My Soul" is, after all, the same blinkin' song. If there's one chief distinction, it's

that Steven Bochco didn't track her down to sing it on *L.A. Law*, and David E. Kelley *did* do that very thing for *Ally*.

That Vonda got delivered the promised land of *Ally* was the result of that perseverance thing at work again.

Vonda, you see, was (and is) always playing. Lugging around her keyboard, or so the Horatio Alger tale goes, from small-potatoes gig to small-potatoes gig in Los Angeles and New York. It made for some dreary nights (and dreary tips), but it also proved to be a fabulous, if roundabout, way to network.

In the early 1980s, actor Peter Horton (*thirtysomething*) palled around with the guitar player in Vonda's band. At the time, Horton was married to future A-list movie star Michelle Pfeiffer. Pfeiffer became a fan of Vonda's music.

Also in the mid-1980s: Future TV titan David E. Kelley was a writer for *L.A. Law*. He got dragged to a Vonda show. He became a Vonda fan.

Cut to 1997: Michelle Pfeiffer and David E. Kelley are now married. Vonda fan Pfeiffer takes Vonda fan Kelley to see (who else?) Vonda at one of her umpteenth L.A. gigs. Kelley's professionally intrigued. He asks for a CD. The next day he calls. Asks club veteran Vonda to play club veteran Vonda on a new show he's cooking up called . . . (please allow for an appropriate Paul Harvey–length dramatic pause here) . . . *Ally McBeal*.

"At first, I was like, 'Yea, I'm going to make a couple of thousand of dollars,'" she told Associated Press. "It was a job and such an honor to be asked by David."

The coolest part of the gig was that Vonda was not just going to be lip-syncing any old background music in a bar

setting; she was going to be lip-syncing *her* music, augmented by an ample catalog of Kelley-suggested 1960s and 1970s oldies. (Up until that point, Vonda didn't do covers.)

In the end, Vonda couldn't have fathomed a greater career boost. The *Ally* pilot turned out to be as much a vehicle for two of Vonda's little-known albums (*The Radical Light* and 1996's *It's Good Eve*) as it was for Calista Flockhart or any of the series' other stars.

Kelley made frequent use of Vonda cuts like "Maryland" and "Neighborhood" and made a theme song of "Searchin' My Soul"—to the eternal discomfort of music critics who slammed the treacly piece as having "an appeal even thinner than Calista Flockhart" (*Entertainment Weekly*).

Journalists could snipe all they wanted. For once, Vonda didn't need to pray for good reviews in order convince the record industry of her continued worth. She had the concerted strength of America's Nielsen families behind her. The easy-to-access primetime format turned out to be the perfect forum for Vonda's easy-to-digest pop-folky tunes. *Ally* was her *Live at Red Rocks*, her *Live at the Acropolis*—to invoke the names of PBS music specials starring John Tesh and Yanni, respectively. Like those two multimedia wizards, Vonda proved the undeniable power of as-seen-on-TV music.

For her accomplishment, she became the proverbial twenty-year overnight success.

"I know this sounds corny, but this is a real example of not giving up on your dreams and believing in myself," she told *TVGen*.

A couple weeks after that February 1998 interview, the example got better: Sony Music acquired the rights to the

Ally TV soundtrack for more than $2 million. By April, "Searchin' My Soul" was a radio hit. By May, the soundtrack was a certified gold record with more than 500,000 units sold (and counting . . . up to 1.7 million at year's end). By *Ally*'s spring hiatus, Vonda was booked on a coast-to-coast tour, with stops on *Live with Regis and Kathie Lee* and *The Tonight Show* included. By the fall of 1998, Vonda was back on *Ally*, this time with her face and name in the opening credits—just like the rest of the stars, even if her route to that place ensured that she was profoundly *unlike* the rest of the stars.

"I've gone from playing to thirty-five people in a dive to being seen by tens of millions of people every Monday," she said in *USA Today*.

The next performer who turns that trick will be the second.

Vonda Shepard—Discography

SOLO

Songs from 'Ally McBeal' (1998; Sony)
1. "Searchin' My Soul"
2. "Ask the Lonely"
3. "Don't Walk Away Renee"
4. "Hooked on a Feeling"
5. "You Belong to Me"
6. "The Wildest Times of the World"
7. "Someone Like You"
8. "The End of the World"
9. "Tell Him"
10. "Neighborhood"

11. "Will You Marry Me?"
12. "It's in His Kiss (The Shoop-Shoop Song)"
13. "I Only Want to Be with You"
14. "Maryland"

It's Good Eve (1996; Vesper Alley)
  1. "Maryland"
  2. "A Lucky Life"
  3. "Grain of Sand"
  4. "The Wildest Times of the World"
  5. "Like a Hemisphere"
  6. "Naivete"
  7. "Long Term Boyfriend"
  8. "Every Now & Then"
  9. "Mischief & Control"
10. "Hotel Room View"
11. "This Steady Train"
12. "Serious Richard"

Radical Light (1992; Reprise)
  1. "Searchin' My Soul"
  2. "The Radical Light"
  3. "100 Tears Away"
  4. "Wake Up the House"
  5. "Clean Rain"
  6. "Dreamin'"
  7. "Good to Yourself"
  8. "Love Will Come and Go"
  9. "Out on the Town"
10. "Cartwheels"

Vonda Shepard (1989; Reprise)
1. "Don't Cry Ilene"
2. "He Ain't with Me"
3. "Baby, Don't You Break My Heart Slow"
4. "Hold Out"
5. "Looking for Something"
6. "I Shy Away"
7. "I've Been Here Before"
8. "A New Marilyn"
9. "Say the Words"
10. "La Journee"
11. "Jam Karet (Life Is Elastic)"

COMPILATION

Pooh's Grand Adventure (1997)—Vonda track (duet with
  Barry Coffing): "Wherever You Are (End Title)"

Putumayo Presents: Travel the World (1997)—Vonda track:
  "Maryland"

Putumayo Presents: Women's Work (1996)—Vonda track:
  "Maryland"

OTHER

Greatest Hits and More: Let Me Show You (Dan Hill; 1993)—
  Vonda track (duet with Dan Hill): "Can't We Try"

Dan Hill (Dan Hill; 1987)—Vonda track (duet with Dan
  Hill): "Can't We Try"

Chapter 11

The Cousin Olivers

They are the well-intentioned newcomers thrust into a veteran, up-and-running series. Their mission: To help keep the series up-and-running. Their curse: their namesake, Cousin Oliver, he of Brady Bunch *infamy. The littlest "fake" Brady reminds all future Cousin Olivers how difficult the task ahead is. How tricky it is to ingratiate yourself to show-me audiences. When it works, you're Blair Underwood on* L.A. Law. *When it doesn't, you're back to square one—you're Cousin Oliver, the bad-luck kid. Until everything gets sorted out, you get a contract— but not your name in the opening credits.*

PORTIA DE ROSSI
(NELLE PORTER)

This is the way getting a TV gig works: (1) You get the gig; (2) Your boss (i.e., the network) lets everyone (i.e., the press) know you got the gig; (3) Your boss tells you to get your tail out there and charm everyone (i.e., the press, again). All this, likely before you've shot a foot of film. To make TV, you gotta sell TV.

In the summer of 1998, Portia de Rossi was selling TV. With a great angle.

You see, not only was de Rossi hired to play a lawyer on the sophomore season of *Ally McBeal*, she is (get this!) a former law school student in her non-TV life (if such a thing exists).

"I wanted to live in L.A. and be an attorney," de Rossi told *TV Guide*.

And now, thanks to *Ally*? She lives in Los Angeles—and *plays* an attorney.

"That's a lot more fun than actually being [one]," she said to the magazine.

Ladies and gentlemen, it doesn't get any better than that.

If de Rossi's got any more choice anecdotes in her files, she'll be in business a long time.

See, even as the seasoned *Ally* players (especially Calista Flockhart) try to separate themselves from their characters, patiently protest that they are not their characters, everybody else (the audience, the media, various unaligned parties) wants to buy into the dream that they *are* their characters.

It's a silly fascination, yeah, but judging by our appetite for such things, it's *our* fascination. Matt Damon just can't tell us to go see him *pretend* to play poker in *Rounders*. Matt Damon has to assure us that he played cards *for real* in the World Series of poker. Like it matters. Like it matters if he knows two of a kind from a flush.

Well, know this: It *matters*.

In fact, never, ever underestimate what matters to a nation that has demanded *Entertainment Tonight* replenish its

populace with pipin' fresh "info-tainment" stories, day in, day out, ever since the first Reagan administration.

So, as for the new kid on the *Ally* docket—Portia de Rossi? She better get used to the *My Character, Myself* bit, even if it is starting to drive her costars a little batty.

To help you conduct your own "Is de Rossi Really Nelle Porter?" investigation, here's some background:

AUSTRALIAN-BORN PORTIA DE ROSSI LEFT HER ACCENT DOWN UNDER TO PLAY ICY *ALLY* ATTORNEY NELLE PORTER—A NEWCOMER FOR SEASON NO. 2.
© SUE SCHNEIDER/FLOWER CHILDREN LTD.

The Early Years: De Rossi was born in Australia. (Like longtime Aussie resident Mel Gibson, she has long since become adept at ditching the Down Under accent.) Her birth-date's a bit of a tricky thing to nail down, although most sources reported her as twenty-four at the time of the *Ally* casting. For what it's worth, one biography claimed her given name was the very un–Portia de Rossi–like moniker of Mandy Rogers.

The Early Dreams: Well, there was that law thing, of course. To become a legal eagle was an early goal. As a kid (a pretty serious one), she abstained from TV—with one excep-tion: *L.A. Law*, the series where David E. Kelley got his start as a writer-producer. (Hey! . . . Another great story!)

She made good on the legal-eagle ambitions—to a point. She enrolled in law school in her native Melbourne.

Stayed there a year. Then got a bite (a second, and a third) about an audition from the makers of *Sirens*, the 1994 arthouse skin flick starring Hugh Grant and an assortment of model types, including real-life model-type Elle MacPherson. De Rossi gave in to the producers' hounding, auditioned, and won the role of Giddy. It was a bit, but it was big enough to leave her smitten with acting. So much for law; now de Rossi wanted to be a thespian. (Not unlike Kelley forsaking his own promising law career for scriptwriting.

Wait, could it be? Yet *another* tie-in anecdote? Some people are just blessed.)

The Early Career: De Rossi moved to Hollywood in 1994. Work followed. Weird work. First, she landed a role in the Fox sitcom *Too Something*. The comedy, bound for the 1995–96 season, was built around Eric Schaeffer and Donal Lardner Ward, two New York guys who turned private obsessions into cinema with the autobiographical *My Life's in Turnaround* (1993). What barely worked on the big screen worked even less on the small screen. The show was pulled in a month—ostensibly put on ice until a magical new title could be found.

De Rossi's second "major" TV gig was for the equally dubious *Nick Freno: Licensed Teacher*, which during its two-year run on the WB (1996–98) was known best (if at all) as The Show That Nobody Watched. De Rossi was cast as Elana Lewis, an instructor in the school-based kiddie sitcom. She wasn't long for the show—but then, the show wasn't long for the air, either. At least she got out before impact.

The Breakthrough: In 1997, she went from teacher to student, as a sorority sister in the horror hit *Scream 2*. It was far from a major role, but it seemed to help her turn a corner; in a short time, she was landing a score of indie movie roles and was cast on *Ally*.

That's the story so far. So the question, again: Is Portia de Rossi *really* Nelle Porter? Depends.

Based on quasi-scientific Internet fan reaction, the early reaction to de Rossi's Frigidaire-model attorney was chilly. For audiences to take to the character, Nelle was going to have to defrost—and de Rossi was going to have to become Nelle.

In viewers' eyes, anyway.

Portia de Rossi—Selected Credits

FILM

American Intellectuals (upcoming)
A Breed Apart (upcoming)
The Invisibles (upcoming)
Toby's Story (upcoming)—Jennifer
Girl (upcoming)—Carla
Scream 2 (1997)—Sorority Sister Murphy
Sirens (1994)—Giddy

TV

Veronica's Closet (NBC; guest star, 10/30/97)—Carolyn
Nick Freno: Licensed Teacher (Fox; series regular, 1996)—
    Elana Lewis
Too Something (Fox; 1995)—Maria Hunter

LUCY LIU
(LING WOO)

Lucy Liu got work. TV guest shots. The odd failed series (namely, CBS's ill-fated 1996–97 Rhea Perlman vehicle, *Pearl*). Movie bits. Work she had. What she didn't have was *the role*.

Signed to a deal with *Ally* a few episodes into Season No. 2, Liu, just maybe, got her crack at *the role*.

A 1986 graduate of Manhattan's Stuyvesant High School (where the notable-alum scale ranges from star—Paul Reiser of *Mad About You* fame—to outcast—ex–President Clinton advisor Dick Morris of toe-sucking infamy), Liu pursued studies at the University of Michigan. Acting gigs started to proliferate in her mid-twenties, when she popped up on stuff like *Home Improvement* playing Woman #3. Maybe not the most stimulating stuff for a person fluent in Mandarin Chinese, but it pays the bills. Lengthens the résumé.

In those early parts, she was billed by her full name, Lucy Alexis Liu. By the time she appeared on *Ally*, debuting in a September 1998 episode titled "They Eat Horses, Don't They?" she was down to Lucy Liu—an interesting phenomenon considering the series is TV's leading safe haven for actors with three-word names.

On *Ally*, Liu was cast as Ling Woo, a client who arrived in tow with new attorney Nelle Porter. With subtlety forever scarce on the series, it was no surprise to learn that Liu's Ling was a steely character who managed (imagine!) a steel factory.

If Liu can overcome that groan-inducing handicap, she just might be long for the *Ally* universe. If she's not, well, at least it was more work.

Lucy Liu — Selected Credits

FILM

City of Industry (1997)—Cathi Rose
Gridlock'd (1997)—Cee-Cee
Jerry Maguire (1996)—Former Girlfriend

TV

NYPD Blue (ABC; guest star, 4/15/97)—Amy Chu
Pearl (CBS; series regular, 1996)—Amy
The X-Files (Fox; guest star, 3/29/96)—Kim
L.A. Law (NBC; guest star, 10/28/93)—Foreign
  Correspondent

Chapter 12

The In-laws

They live out of town. Sometimes you see them; sometimes you don't. Sometimes they stick around; sometimes they drift away. When they visit, they bring presents (a beloved catchphrase, an endearing character quirk). When they leave, they leave you wanting a little more of their time. Unless they are the Dancing Baby, in which case, they're the annoying relative you just can't lose.

THE DANCING BABY
(THE DANCING BABY)

Some people like the Dancing Baby. There is ample proof of this. There is, for instance, the Dancing Baby necktie. And the Dancing Baby screensaver. And the Dancing Baby T-shirt. And, of course, *The Official Dancing Baby CD*.

The wise manufacturing community distributed these products because, presumably, they believed that some (many?) people liked the Dancing Baby enough to buy anything on which he/she/it lent his/her/its creepy, mottled little face.

And, lo, they were right.

Dancing Baby T-shirts disappeared from shelves. The Dancing Baby music CD moved 300,000 copies during its first four weeks of release. Captains of industry said, "Please, let us turn this magical Dancing Baby into a ready-made Halloween costume, complete with a line of adult sizes."

Then, the capper: The Dancing Baby got a guest spot on *Rosie O'Donnell*. Then, the second capper: The Dancing Baby got a national commercial for Blockbuster Video.

All this was, again, ample proof that some people like the Dancing Baby.

Which is kind of funny because the Dancing Baby is stupid.

There is not ample proof of this latter statement, of course. Just a gut feeling.

Far from impugning the Dancing Baby's good name, it should be noted here that the computerized tot has enriched the lives of millions—or at least the hundreds (thousands?) who cashed in on his/her/its popularity. Among those profiting from the Dancing Baby phenomena: *Ally McBeal*.

It turned out that the sluggish-moving, ethereal-looking animated diaper-wearer was the perfect foil for David E. Kelley's title character—a muddled-minded, ethereal-looking twentysomething skirt-wearer. By itself, *Ally* was a show of many gimmicks, lacking the essential signature gimmick. By itself, the Dancing Baby was a creature of the Internet, a star of the vast but cultish cyberworld. Matched together onscreen, they conquered the popular culture.

Plus, the Dancing Baby was a much better catch for Ally than that Billy guy Kelley usually had his heroine chasing.

All of this doesn't make the Dancing Baby any less stupid. But it makes you admire the guy/gal/thing a little more.

Certainly, the baby's rise to celebrity status was remarkable. It—and for the sake of brevity, and until such time that a proper sex ID can be made, Dancing Baby will heretofore be referred to in this text with the pronoun *it*. (Although, frankly, here's betting the thing's a boy. There's no way Ally McBeal, with the drama-queen love life fit for a junior-high-schooler, spends that much energy fretting over a girl.)

In any case, *it* hails from humble origins. Dancing Baby began life as a demo model—the spawn of animators at a computer graphics studio, name of Kinetix. In a fable that mirrors the old Reese's Peanut Butter Cup ad campaign (wherein the candy is invented when peanut-butter-toting party A collides with chocolate-toting party B and their foodstuffs intermingle—thereby creating an accidental, but magical, product), Baby was one of several characters on the demo for Kinetix's Character Studio 3-D animation software. According to animator Ron Lussier's straight-from-the-horse's mouth account on the Official Dancing Baby Web Page, the demo featured a chimp character, an alien, a woman and a monster, as well. Also included were motion files that demonstrated how Character Studio could get your creations to do ballet, even the cha-cha. In 1996, as Lussier explains it, the baby and the cha-cha were wedded—and the world as we knew it ended.

"A few people were talking about how disturbing this dance motion was on the baby . . . in an interesting way," Lussier wrote. "It seems to really bug some people."

Indeed.

But, to be fair, it also seemed to fascinate people, too. How else to explain the explosion of Baby Cha-Cha? In late 1996, a version of the dancing tot got duped and copied and circulated through the Internet community. He, er, *it* was on its way.

Soon, Baby Cha-Cha was boogying on Web pages the world over—sometimes it danced to B. J. Thomas's "Hooked on a Feeling" as rendered by 1970s one-hit wonders Blue Suede, sometimes it grooved to the Bee Gees, or any other number of tunes. Kinetix was cool about letting the thing run wild. As long as the company got credit, you, too, could add Baby Cha-Cha to your homepage.

"We're really tickled how it has taken off," Jeff Yates of Kinetix told *USA Today* in 1998. "It's a wonderful way to get the word out about the product."

Okay, so Baby Cha-Cha was all over the place. He even had his own spin-off character, Drunken Baby—the result of two other files on the Character Studio demo being merged. But what next? It *was* just a computer program, after all. It wasn't like it could get booked on *Rosie O'Donnell*.

Or could it? . . .

In 1997, Kelley was pounding out an *Ally* script when he got a look at the Net's ubiquitous baby.

"He loved it," co-executive producer Jeffrey Kramer said in *People*. "It was a perfect illustration of Ally's biological clock."

And so, on the January 5, 1998, episode, "Cro-Magnon," Baby Cha-Cha, heretofore to be known as the Dancing Baby, made its primetime debut.

As Kramer noted, Kelley used the silent, solemn-looking newborn to stalk his heroine. When the warlike "ooga-chaka"

chant of Blue Suede's "Hooked on a Feeling" sounded, Ally was in for it.

By the end of the episode, an extra-special TV moment had been minted: a pajama-clad grown woman cutting a rug (or, rather, hardwood floor) with the computer-animated baby. Maybe it wasn't *Requiem for a Heavyweight*, but it was . . . cute.

The Dancing Baby—and *Ally*—had it made.

That the series would begin to suffer from a terminal case of the cutes from this point on could not have been foreseen. One could only guess, perhaps, that a baby who looked like the gassed-out ghost of the Nepal chemical disaster might not be the shiniest of good-luck charms.

As far as the Dancing Baby was concerned, of course, everything was fine. Within four months of its first *Ally* appearance, it released its own CD (complete with four— count 'em, four—remix versions of "Hooked on a Feeling.") Within a couple more months, there was the *Rosie* spot, the Blockbuster gig and the talk of the Halloween-costume line. And now, your very own Dancing Baby flip book!

Yes, the Dancing Baby was more than fine. Not even the vow of *Ally* producers to go cold turkey in Season No. 2, could derail its steaming-ahead, steam-engine status. (Nothing personal against the Baby, they said. Just time to move on to other stuff.)

No matter, Dancing Baby was priced to move.

It was *still* stupid. It was *still* a soulless computer program. It was *still* a glorified Pet Rock with killer demographic appeal (the master stroke being the oldies soundtrack, proving again that from *The Big Chill* to brownie commercials nothing sells quite like baby-boomer nostalgia). But it was what it was.

Whatever viewers projected on it, whatever the makers of *Ally* projected on it . . . Well, that was their collective problem. The Dancing Baby, 3-D or no, didn't do introspection.

DYAN CANNON
(WHIPPER CONE)

It's the prototypical career track of women in Hollywood. One day you're best known as the nubile wife (later ex-wife) of a dapper movie star (Cary Grant). The next you're best known for your wattle—"a fleshy flap of skin hanging from the throat of certain birds or lizards," as the dictionary oh-so-delicately puts it.

Dyan Cannon, like other actresses of her era, is much more than the sum of her famous lovers and aging skin, of course. But Hollywood rarely gives its women credit for anything else.

It simply doesn't let them forget their age.

In Cannon's case, *Ally McBeal* didn't really, either.

Sure, she was cast as one of its regularly presiding judges, Jennifer "Whipper" Cone. Sure, Whipper was supposed to be a strong woman. Sure, Whipper was supposed to have a young lover—Greg Germann's peculiar, wattle-fingering Richard Fish.

But underneath it all? Whipper was supposed to be the show's resident *older* woman.

Next stop: Double Standard City.

If Jurassic Jack Nicholson romances a mostly unlined Helen Hunt (see: *As Good As It Gets*), the story line is about his character's attempt to win her love. It's not about his attempts, as a borderline senior citizen, to win the love of a much younger woman.

He's a guy first; an older guy, second (if at all).

On *Ally*, as per the dynamic of Hollywood, Whipper—despite the robes and law talk—was an older woman first; a judge, lover and plain old, regular woman, second. Fish's romance of Whipper was not about the conflict of a lawyer in love with a member of the judiciary branch. It was about the

WHAT KIND OF SIXTYSOME-THING IS DYAN CANNON? THE KIND WHO'S STILL GOT A MIDRIFF—AND ISN'T SHY ABOUT SHOWING IT OFF.
© ALBERT L. ORTEGA/FLOWER CHILDREN LTD.

kinky vibe of a young man in love with an older woman.

The producers set the bait. The audience bought it—hook, line and wattle.

Dyan Cannon made the most of the same-old, same-old setup. She boarded the *Ally* bus and took the Whipper thing for a ride—scoring more ink, attention and respect than she had in years. She gracefully accepted her role as chief reassurer to the rapidly graying baby-boomer masses, telling them what they so desperately wanted to believe: Getting older = getting better.

"There's a lot you go through as an older woman that we need to learn to applaud instead of downgrade," Cannon said in *TV Guide*, the party line down pat.

That Cannon needed to be rediscovered as a sort-of poster girl for aging was yet another testament to how shab-

bily we treat our elders, both men and women. Really, why *did* Cannon need to be rediscovered? Save for brief spells, she never went away. And even during those lower-profile periods, she could be spotted courtside at Los Angeles Lakers basketball games. You probably remember her. She was the "older woman" a couple aisles away from "leading man" Jack Nicholson.

Dyan Cannon was born January 4, 1937, in Tacoma, Washington—giving her all of four months' seniority on Smilin' Jack. To be accurate, it was Samille Diane Friesen who was born in Tacoma. Dyan Cannon was born in Hollywood. She arrived there with a beauty-queen résumé (she'd been crowned Miss West Seattle in her native rainy-day state) and modest ambitions (she wanted to be a model). A contract with fading movie studio MGM made her an actress. Sort of. She didn't get much work outside of beach-bunny guest spots on beach-bunny TV shows, including the short-lived series, *Malibu Run*.

Sometimes, though, even short-lived series can serve a higher purpose—as was the case with Cannon and *Malibu*. The story goes that Hollywood legend Cary Grant noticed Cannon on an episode of *Malibu Run* and pursued the blonde, who was thirty-five years his junior.

What the sublime star of sublime movies like *The Philadelphia Story* was doing sampling something called *Malibu Run* has never been adequately explained. Think of it— this was before the age of zap-friendly remote controls. You couldn't just zip back and forth from channel to channel, not with lightning precision, anyway. Ol' Cary would really have to make an effort to bump into something called *Malibu Run*.

In any case, the unlikely duo soon became a live-in duo. By July 1965, they were married. It was Cannon's biggest role to date: Mrs. Cary Grant #4.

In 1966, they welcomed a child—daughter Jennifer (best known today for playing one of Ian Ziering's TV girlfriends on *Beverly Hills 90210.*) Grant bowed out of his illustrious movie career to spend more time with the newborn.

Despite appearances—young mom, healthy baby, doting dad—all was not well at the movie-star household. In 1968, Cannon filed for divorce. And not just any divorce—one that accused Grant of "cruel and inhuman manner" and depicted their life as a "terrifying, unromantic nightmare." Spats over child custody followed. It was not a pretty time but it left Cannon open to accept her second biggest role to date: Free Woman.

As such, she blossomed. She earned a Best Supporting Actress Oscar nomination for her first major film role, 1969's rumpled-bedsheets comedy, *Bob & Carol & Ted & Alice.* High-profile film work followed: 1972's *The Anderson Tapes* with Sean Connery, 1973's *Shamus* with Burt Reynolds and *The Last of Sheila* with James Mason, also from 1973.

In 1978, she backed up Warren Beatty in the hit comedy remake *Heaven Can Wait,* and pulled down her second Academy Award nod for Best Supporting Actress. Once again she didn't win, but Cannon could cope. She'd already claimed one of the shiny bald guys. At the 1977 ceremonies, she won an Oscar for her 1976 live-action short, *Number One.* The former bathing-suit queen who wanted to be a model had matured into an award-winning Hollywood multihyphenate: writer-producer-editor-director.

By this point, the MO of the all-new Dyan Cannon was clear: She was cool. Like the way she reportedly installed soundproof padding in her home following the Grant breakup (the better with which to undergo primal-scream therapy). Like the way she made peace with Grant well before his death in 1986. Like the way her second divorce, from attorney Stanley Fimburg, involved a squabble over Lakers season tickets. Like the way she struggled for years to make (and write and direct and star in) the woman-on-the-verge drama, *The End of Innocence* (1991)—even if the thing did turn out to be a bomb. Like the way she hosted an installment of *The Muppet Show*.

Cool.

Cannon first appeared on *Ally* in the Season No. 1 episode "Compromising Positions." It was too soon to know then that *Ally* was on its way to becoming *Ally*: Certified "It" Show, or that Cannon was on her way to becoming Cannon: Certified Rediscovery. The actress, in fact, only signed to appear in one show.

But by Episode No. 5, "One Hundred Tears Away," she was back.

Dyan Cannon, wattle and all, is not so easily dismissed.

Dyan Cannon—Selected Credits

FILM

Out to Sea (1997)—Liz LaBreche
8 Heads in a Duffel Bag (1997)—Annette Bennett
That Darn Cat (1997)—Mrs. Flint
The Pickle (1993)—Ellen Stone

The End of Innocence (1991)—Stephanie (also writer-director)
Caddyshack II (1988)—Elizabeth Pearce
Author! Author! (1982)—Alice Detroit
Deathtrap (1982)—Myra Bruhl
Honeysuckle Rose (1980)—Viv Bonham
Revenge of the Pink Panther (1978)—Simone Legree
Heaven Can Wait (1978)—Julia Farnsworth
Number One (1976; short)—(writer-director-producer-editor)
The Last of Sheila (1973)—Christine
Shamus (1973)—Alexis
The Anderson Tapes (1972)—Ingrid
Doctors' Wives (1971)—Lorrie Dellman
The Love Machine (1971)—Judith Austin
Such Good Friends (1971)—Julie Messinger
Bob & Carol & Ted & Alice (1969)—Alice Henderson

TV

The Practice (ABC; guest star, 1/5/98)—Whipper Cone
The Naked Truth (ABC; guest star, 11/29/95)—Mitzi
The Muppet Show (Syndicated; guest host, 1979)—herself
Saturday Night Live (NBC; guest host, 5/15/76)—herself
Medical Center (CBS; guest star, 1969)—Elinor Crawford
Gunsmoke (CBS; guest star, 2/19/64)—Ivy Norton
Malibu Run (CBS; 1961)

STEVE AND ERIC COHEN
(THE DANCING TWINS)

These are the other Cohen brothers of Hollywood. The first,
with apologies to Steve and Eric, are the sound-alike Coens—

Joel and Ethan, the guys with the Oscars for writing 1996's "Gee, people in Minnesota have funny accents" comedy, *Fargo*.

As for the other Cohen brothers—no Oscars there. No critical acclaim. No movie-star marriages to Frances McDormand. But, hey, they've got their own Web site (http://members.aol.com/allytwins)!

And that's not bad, considering the Cohen brothers were inspired to launch their own corner of cyberspace based on nonspeaking, nonstarring, nonregular roles on a single primetime TV series.

Yes, these Cohens are *Ally McBeal*'s Dancing Twins. (Not to be confused with *Ally McBeal*'s Dancing Baby.)

To explain the Dancing Twins would be an insult to the Cohens' still-ticking, fifteen-minute fame clock. Everybody knows the Dancing Twins, right? Jeez, pretty soon you'll be able to buy your own Dancing Twins T-shirt, your own Dancing Twins poster and, of course, your own Dancing Twins dance instruction video.

The Dancing Twins are, simply: The Dancing Twins— Multimedia Phenomenon.

They're a testament to the press *Ally* commandeered during its freshman season. The first thing you know, thirty-something Stanford grads Steve and Eric Cohen inexplicably turn up in the September 8, 1997, pilot. (They were just *there*—in the nightclub setting where the Cage/Fish lawyers hang—sporting matching shirts and dorky disco moves.) The second thing you know, they're being interviewed by a daily newspaper (the *Toronto Sun*) and talking about how they hope to get their own spin-off series.

"Or maybe we'll go straight to feature films," Steve or Eric told the newspaper (the *Sun* writer confessed she didn't know which twin was which). "We have a script for a juggling movie we've written with a friend of ours in which we play the world's greatest jugglers."

But of course.

Prior to their sporadic *Ally* gigs, the Cohens juggled their way into the movies *Batman Forever* (1995) and *Batman and Robin* (1997), and onto TV (*Seinfeld, Mad About You, Baywatch*). As a solo commodity, Steve worked as Jim Carrey's double in *The Cable Guy* (1996), as well as the afore-mentioned *Batman Forever*.

Strangely, their résumé is bereft of ads for twin-friendly Doublemint gum.

No matter, the Cohens are beyond that sort of stunt casting now. They're built for the future. They're "multi-skilled entertainers," the Official Dancing Twins Web site tells us, ". . .who could have gone on to do anything."

And they have! Mastering the unicycle, the accordion, plate-spinning and darts.

Anyone mention yet that they each type 100-plus words a minute? (Duly noted.)

Somehow, with all these plates spinning, they manage to squeeze in time for choreography, too. Yes, the Cohens map out their very own dance moves for their very own *Ally* appearances.

As Steve said in an *Ultimate TV* online chat: "The first time we were told to dance, we choreographed the first move [in] just five minutes."

Impossible?

Everything is possible in a world where Andy Warhol's 1960s-tinged vision of the cult of celebrity doesn't quite cut it anymore.

Steve and Eric Cohen—Selected Credits

(All below appearances were as featured jugglers.)

FILM

Baby Geniuses (upcoming)
Batman and Robin (1997)
Batman Forever (1995)

TV

Baywatch
Mad About You
Seinfeld

TATE DONOVAN
(RONALD CHEANIE)

Tate Donovan played one of the *Ally* guys—the first in a series of hapless boyfriend types (his character, Ronald Cheanie, had a thing about kissing, as in, he didn't like to— not Ally, anyway) who sort-of courted the equally confused series heroine during Season No. 1.

Call it typecasting.

Donovan, a peer and former costar to the likes of Matt Damon, Michael J. Fox and Eric Stoltz, is less known for his

own work and better known as The Boyfriend. First of Sandra (*Speed*) Bullock. Then of Jennifer (*Friends*) Aniston.

At least the *Ally* relationship got him decent solo screen time. Such are the small victories one must extract from the heaven that is Hollywood. And so it goes.

Born September 25, 1963, in New York City, Donovan hails from a large (six kids—he's the youngest) Irish-American clan. Kind of like the one (down to the NYC setting) he hailed from on the NBC drama series *Trinity*, which premiered in the fall of 1998.

Call it typecasting.

Sort of.

On *Trinity*, Donovan played a priest. In real life, acting was his calling. He studied theater at the University of Southern California. Started getting work as a baby-faced twentysomething. Scored one-shot tube gigs on everything from *Family Ties* to *Magnum, P.I.*

The first major film role came in 1986's *SpaceCamp*, about a bunch of kids who (uh-oh!) accidentally launch themselves into orbit on the space shuttle. Think a high-minded, big-budget *Far Out Space Nuts* with really bad timing—the movie was released just months after the very real space shuttle *Challenger* crashed and burned on live TV. *SpaceCamp*'s failure was more a blow to the big-screen dreams of top-line star Lea Thompson than to supporting player Donovan. He went to work (and work and work); Thompson returned to punish us all for the slight with the NBC "comedy" series *Caroline in the City*.

It's Donovan's luck (or plight) that his next major film outing brought him attention not for his work (even though

OUTFITTED IN A TUX, TATE DONOVAN LOOKS FIT FOR A WEDDING CAKE—THE SORT OF QUALITY THAT MAKES HIM QUINTESSENTIAL TV BOYFRIEND MATERIAL.

© SUE SCHNEIDER/FLOWER CHILDREN LTD.

it was his debut as The Star), but for his costar. The movie was *Love Potion No. 9*, a forgettable 1991 comedy remembered only when somebody wants to cite the early, lesser opuses of Sandra Bullock. Bullock played Donovan's love interest, onscreen and off. The two dated for a few years. Then things *Speed*-ed away.

Next came projects like the 1995–96 Fox sitcom *Partners* (his first TV series, with Jon Cryer) and *Inside Monkey Zetterland*, a little-seen film about the life (such as it is) of a struggling screenwriter that earned him a 1994 Independent Spirit Award nomination for best supporting actor.

Still, the highest-profile project Donovan undertook during this period was a coupling with Jennifer Aniston, once a regular working actress herself, but as of 1994, a "Must-See TV" superstar.

Donovan "is unbelievably sensitive and funny and warm," Aniston told *USA Weekend* in 1997. "He's like a spirit."

By the following summer she was dating Brad Pitt.

And so it goes.

Tate Donovan—Selected Credits

FILM

Murder at 1600 (1997)—Kyle Neil

Hercules (1997)—Hercules (voice)

Inside Monkey Zetterland (1993)—Brian Zetterland

Ethan Frome (1993)—Reverend Smith

Equinox (1992)—Richie Nunn

Love Potion No. 9 (1991)—Paul Matthews

Memphis Belle (1990)—Luke

Dead-Bang (1989)—John Burns

Clean and Sober (1988)—Donald Towle

SpaceCamp (1986)—Kevin

No Small Affair (1984)—Bob

TV

Trinity (NBC; 1998–)—Kevin McCallister

Friends (NBC; guest star, five episodes from 1/29/98 to 4/16/98)—Joshua

Homicide: Life on the Street (NBC; guest star, 2/7/97)—Greg Kellerman

Partners (Fox; series regular, 1995–96)—Owen

Rising Son (TNT; 1990; TV movie)—Des

Magnum, P.I. (CBS; guest star, 1/9/86)—Robin Masters's nephew

Family Ties (NBC; guest star, one episode in 1984)—Clancy

MICHAEL EASTON
(GLENN)

The cult of *Ally McBeal* is not a new phenomenon to Michael Easton.

Easton got a membership to the *Ally* charter group by virtue of dropping his robe as Glenn, the (Very) Well-

Endowed Male Model. The three-episode gig was all very nice, and certainly upped his grandma profile (defined by the number of gray-haired grandmas who can correctly ID a pop-culture personality). But, fact is, Michael Easton was a thriving cult figure with or without *Ally*.

As an actor, there are two jobs you can land that will ensure you, if nothing else, a lifetime of all-expenses-paid invites to fawning fan conventions.

You can (1) get cast on a *Star Trek* show; or (2) get cast on a daytime soap.

Easton made good on the second half of that mandate in 1989, when the New York–based, would-be playwright (born February 15, 1967) was cast in NBC's *Days of Our Lives*.

The son of Irish immigrants, Easton, then twenty-two, was discovered by a network talent scout who happened upon a play he had written—and decided to costar in because he was, well, cheap.

"I asked [the scout] how she liked the play," Easton told the *Hollywood Reporter*. "And she said, 'Possibly the worst play I've seen in New York in eight years. But you're not a bad actor.'"

Fast-forward a couple months and Easton was on the West Coast doing the studly soap thing as studly Tanner Scofield on *Days*, a show that is perhaps soapdom's leading exporter of Extremely Devoted Fans. Easton had it made. As long as he didn't mind forever being called "Tanner" by reality-challenged viewers.

Easton didn't wait to see if his identity would be lost in the soaps. He departed the never-ending daytime drama in 1992

and promptly took off for about two years to care for his terminally ill, cancer-stricken mother.

When he got back in the Hollywood game, Easton completed the actor's "don't forget about me" daily double by scoring, in 1995, his first regular primetime series role on Fox's *VR.5.* All right, the thing wasn't *Star Trek,* but it *was* sci-fi, which is close enough. Instead of Klingons and spaceships, *VR.5* focused on virtual reality mumbo-jumbo. It went over as big as that year's ill-fated VR

ALLY GUEST STAR MICHAEL EASTON BETTER GET USED TO IT—UNTIL FURTHER NOTICE, HE'S THE BIG-PENIS GUY. OF COURSE, THAT'S NOT NECESSARILY A BAD THING.
© SUE SCHNEIDER/FLOWER CHILDREN LTD.

film, *Johnny Mnemonic,* starring Keanu Reeves (who played in a band, Dogstar, with Robert Mailhouse, who played Easton's TV brother on *Days* . . . this sort of loopy connectedness being the Hollywood version of virtual reality.)

Another series with fantasy elements, *Two,* ostensibly the flip side of *The Patty Duke Show* (one twin's good—the other twin's *EVIL!*), cemented his rep in the sci-fi world. (His 1998 *Total Recall* series, based on the 1990 Arnold Schwarzenegger film, wasn't going to hurt, either.)

So this *Ally* stuff—this, "Ooh, look, it's the male-model guy!"—couldn't be any worse than being tracked down for an autograph by a middle-aged guy wearing a Fantastic Four T-shirt. In fact, it probably could be better.

"A few more people follow you around the supermarket, checking out your . . . your grocery cart," Easton said on *Entertainment Tonight*, of life after *Ally*.

Easton got the *Ally* job just days after *413 Hope St.*, yet another failed series for Fox (neither a soap nor a sci-fi effort, but a sincere inner-city drama costarring fellow future *Ally* boyfriend, Jesse L. Martin), was canceled in late 1997.

Pleasant work environment in *McBeal*-land or no, as an actor, there's ultimately but one job you can land that will ensure your peace of mind—and that's being your own boss.

To that end, Easton, a published poet, wrote, directed and produced the 1996 short film *Daedalus Is Dead*, starring fellow soap refugee Ami Dolenz (*General Hospital*). Whether Easton's bid to become an in-demand multi-hyphenate (writer-director-actor-whatever) pans out remains to be seen. That his turns in cult TV mean there will always be a glossy for him to sign, a photo op for him to pose for, a speaking engagement for him to accept, seems assured.

It's a living.

Michael Easton—Selected Credits

FILM

Daedalus Is Dead (1996; short)—(writer-director-producer)
Coldfire (1991)—Jake Edwards

TV

The Practice (ABC; guest star, 10/25/98) . . .Blind Date
Total Recall 2070 (Showtime; 1998–)—David Hume
413 Hope St. (Fox; 1997)—Nick Carrington

Two (Syndicated; 1996–97)—Gus McClain/Booth Hubbard
VR.5 (Fox; series regular, 1995)—Duncan
Judith Krantz's 'Dazzle' (CBS; 1995; TV movie)—Nick
Diagnosis: Murder (CBS; guest star, 4/29/94)—Rick
Shadow of a Stranger (NBC; 1992; TV movie)—Shawn
Days of Our Lives (NBC; series regular, 1989–92)—Tanner
    Scofield

PRINT
Eighteen Straight Whiskeys (1997; Bowery Press, poetry)

JESSE L. MARTIN
(DR. GREG BUTTERS)

On *Ally*, Jesse L. Martin was the Normal Boyfriend, Dr. Greg
Butters. Good-looking, sensitive, unattached and bound for
out-of-town.

You had to figure that a profoundly non-dysfunctional
presence like that of the sturdy Martin wasn't long for the
screwed-up *Ally* universe. And he wasn't; Butters was gone in
three episodes. However brief, the exposure was a boon for
Martin, a stage veteran with little prior success in film or TV.

Of course, when you're creating a role in the original
Broadway cast of *Rent*, stuff like not landing the lead in (*theoret-
ical* example) an Olsen twins project, tends not to sting so much.

Rent is where Martin made his first heavy-duty mark.
Following Broadway stints in Serious Actor Plays like *Timon
of Athens* and *The Gentleman Caller* (plus tons of regional theater, and assorted daytime soap bits on *One Life to Live* and

Guiding Light), Martin won the role of Tom Collins in the rock musical's 1995 Off-Broadway debut.

When composer Jonathan Larson's show—Puccini's *La Bohème* set in New York's scummy East Village—moved to Broadway in January 1996, Martin moved with it. And when *Rent* succeeded, Martin succeeded. He got the attention, the good reviews ("performers of both wit and emotional conviction," the *New York Times* said, of Martin and costars) and the career juice that goes with being part of a marketable hit.

As Tom Collins, the math whiz with a Robin Hood bent, Martin was (again) the Normal Boyfriend—the centered guy with the capacity for a centered relationship, HIV-positive status and cross-dressing lover notwithstanding. The role, showcasing his seductive baritone, brought him an Obie Award for the production's Off-Broadway run. By 1997, Martin was in the Hollywood way, signing up for his first regular TV series gig, *413 Hope St.* The show was from comic actor Damon Wayans—*Blankman*'s bid to get serious.

The Wayans production was set at a teen help center in a scummy section of New York City. In short, *413 Hope St.* was supposed to be the kind of place where the low-life kids of *Rent* could snag clean needles. And who better to provide that *Rent* vibe than a *Rent* veteran himself, Jesse L. Martin? (Network TV: Innovative Thinking at Its Best.) In short order, Martin was cast as Antonio, the Normal Married Guy and staff psychologist.

Earnest or no, the drama series, which debuted on Fox in the fall of 1997, was off the air in a matter of months, sending Martin and costar Michael Easton into the clutches of *Ally*.

Martin looked to break out of the Normal Guy mode with a long-planned, one-man show based on the life of troubled singer Marvin Gaye.

Until then, all's—well, normal.

Jesse L. Martin—Selected Credits

FILM
Restaurant (upcoming)—Quincy

TV
413 Hope St. (Fox; series regular, 1997)—Antonio
New York Undercover (Fox; guest star, 3/16/95)—Mustafa

STAGE
Rent (London; 1998)—Tom Collins
Rent (Broadway; 1996)—Tom Collins
Timon of Athens (Broadway; 1993)
The Government Inspector (Broadway; 1993)

MUSIC
Broadway cast album:
Rent (1997; DreamWorks)

TRACEY ULLMAN
(DR. TRACY CLARK)

Tracey Ullman gave *The Simpsons* their big break. Collaborated on a music video with Paul McCartney. Costarred in a movie with Meryl Streep.

TRACEY ULLMAN BACKSTAGE AT THE 1996–97 PRIMETIME EMMY AWARDS—A WINNER FOR HER CULT-FAVORITE HBO SERIES, *TRACEY TAKES ON.*

© SUE SCHNEIDER/FLOWER CHILDREN LTD.

In the scheme of things, urging drippy Ally McBeal to get a life, not to mention a theme song, in the guise of TV-land therapist Dr. Tracy Clark, doesn't jump right out there as, you know: Dream Gig.

But you know what? If there's but one good-citizen contribution that *Ally McBeal* has made to society, it's finding a coast-to-coast primetime job for Ullman, a talent inexplicably confined to cable (her Emmy-winning, HBO sketch comedy show); early, little-seen Fox (her *other* Emmy-winning sketch comedy show); and sporadic movie work.

Born December 30, 1959, in England, Ullman won over her native land before moving stateside with her husband, producer Allan McKeown, in the mid-1980s. One of those annoying, prodigy types, Ullman was a kid actor who worked regularly on the London stage (in productions of *Grease* and *The Rocky Horror Show*), before moving into an equally precocious young adulthood and careers in British TV (with the comedy *Three of a Kind*) and the British pop charts (with her 1983 debut album, *You Broke My Heart in 17 Places*).

First impressions in the United States came with the bubblegum single, "They Don't Know." In 1984, the song cracked the Top Ten; the accompanying video (with the aforementioned Mr. McCartney) attracted attention. But despite that initial blush of success, Ullman was wary of her new homeland.

"They don't want film people who look like real people [in Hollywood]," Ullman told E! Online. "I've never wanted to play straight people on film—never wanted to be the princess. I always wanted to play the ugly sisters."

Hollywood being about as big on ugly-sister projects as it is on uplifting scripts about macroeconomics, Ullman quickly became the ultimate square peg in Showbiz, USA Style.

Sure, there were a few film roles (notably, the 1985 drama *Plenty*, with the aforementioned Ms. Streep), but not much else—until 1987, when then fledgling Fox, hoping to keep the culture police at bay, gave her money to do a TV show.

The Tracey Ullman Show premiered on April 5, 1987, following the prototypical Fox series, *Married . . . With Children*. Thankfully, the residual slime factor was low. Ullman's character-driven sketch comedy was allowed to emerge, its IQ intact. In the end, the show won the upstart network its first-ever Emmy, and launched *The Simpsons*, the jaundiced 'toon family of future hit series and ubiquitous marketing tie-in fame. (The Matt Groening characters got a couple minutes of screentime on most *Ullman* episodes.)

And what was Ullman's reward? Sporadic film work (notably, Woody Allen's 1994 effort, *Bullets Over Broadway*). Not much else.

She returned to sketch comedy in 1996 with *Tracey Takes On . . .* on HBO. A prestige gig, yeah, but—bottom line—a

prestige gig on pay cable. (Which is kind of like going to the trouble of squeezing into a diamond-sparkly ball gown and letting exactly seven people see you in the thing.)

And then, to the semi-rescue: David E. Kelley wrote Ullman into the burgeoning *Ally* empire (and back into primetime view), with the recurring Dr. Clark role, starting in March 1998.

The square peg still grinds. But now it makes a little more noise. Gets a little more notice.

Tracey Ullman—Selected Credits

FILM

Bullets Over Broadway (1994)—Eden Brent
Ready to Wear (1994)—Nina Scant
I Love You to Death (1990)—Rosalie
Jumpin' Jack Flash (1986)—Fiona
Plenty (1985)—Alice Park
Give My Regards to Broad Street (1984)—Sandra

TV

Tracey Takes On . . . (HBO; 1996–)—Star
The Tracey Ullman Show (Fox; 1987–90)—Star/Host

MUSIC

You Broke My Heart in 17 Places (1983; Stiff Records, UK)
     (1984; MCA, USA)
You Caught Me Out (1984; Stiff Records, UK)
Forever: The Best of Tracey (1985; Stiff Records, UK)
The Best of Tracey Ullman (1992; Rhino Records, USA)

PRINT

Tracey Takes On... (1998; companion guide to HBO series, published by Hyperion.)

THE PRACTICE PEOPLE

That David E. Kelley—sharp guy. He goes and mixes and matches his bounty of primetime television shows and, in the process, finagles himself (and his creations) a little extra print. Well, he wins this one. Thanks to Kelley's pollination efforts, no *Ally* discussion is complete without at least a cursory look at its cousin, *The Practice* (ABC, 1997–).

Actually, to continue with the family-tree metaphors, *The Practice* is more like the classic elder sibling—the serious, driven type who gets outshined by the younger, cuter, bouncier baby of the family. The baby, in this example, undeniably being *Ally*. *The Practice* premiered first, got good reviews first, did everything first—outside of introducing the Dancing Twins, becoming a hit and collecting pretty trophies. (*Ally* scored big wins at the 1998 editions of both the Screen Actors Guild and Golden Globe Awards, while *The Practice* got stiffed.)

It wasn't until the 1997–98 Primetime Emmys that the slow, but steady (and serious—*always* serious) *Practice* exacted a small measure of revenge. On that night, it was *The Practice* in the spotlight (named Outstanding Drama Series) and *Ally* in the shadows.

And then the new TV season started and . . . Everything Was Coming Up *Ally*! Again.

DYLAN MCDERMOTT STARS AS
DARK-KNIGHT BOBBY DONNELL
ON *ALLY* SISTER SHOW, *THE
PRACTICE.*
© SUE SCHNEIDER/FLOWER CHILDREN LTD.

Oh, well, there's always the promise of more crossover episodes.

Here's a look at the key *Practice* players who stepped into the la-la land that is *Ally* for the Season No. 1 episode "The Inmates."

Dylan McDermott (**Bobby Donnell**): Tall, dark, handsome. The kind of guy who usually exists only in inanimate-object form atop wedding cakes. *The Practice* is his first TV series. He's a film guy, by way of theater. The onetime flame of *Pretty Woman* Julia Roberts played her husband in the 1990 weepie *Steel Magnolias*. Other credits include *Home for the Holidays* (1995); *Miracle on 34th Street* (1994); *In the Line of Fire* (1993). (He also guested on *Ally*'s Season No. 1 finale, "These Are the Days.")

Camryn Manheim (**Ellenor Frutt**): The all-new Sally ("You really like me!") Field. Her "This one's for the fat girls!" line at the 1997–98 Emmys (she won Outstanding Supporting Actress in a Drama Series) will get quoted back to her as often as her anecdote about how she wore a pair of Fayva shoes to the big night. (Note: That's going to be *a lot*.) Wrote and performed the one-woman play *Wake Up! I'm Fat!* (She got an Obie—an Off-Broadway honor—for that show.) Says she doesn't resent or begrudge *Ally* its success. "We reap some of the benefits of it being such a sensational hit," she told the *Los Angeles Times*. Other credits include *Romy and Michele's High School Reunion* (1997); *Jeffrey* (1995); *David Searching* (1995).

Steve Harris (**Eugene Young**): Plays another of *The Practice's* steady, dedicated attorneys. Gets to play it cool in the big-screen version of *The Mod Squad*, due in 1999. A veteran of primetime drama series in the 1990s, with guest stints on *Homicide: Life on the Street*, *Law & Order* and Kelley's *Chicago Hope*. Other film credits include *The Rock* (1996).

Kelli Williams (**Lindsay Dole**): One-third of *The Practice's* quasi-version of *Ally's* Ally-Billy-Georgia triangle. (Her character has the hots for McDermott's Bobby, who had a fling with Lara Flynn Boyle's Helen Gamble. . . .) Her training for the soapy story line? Well, she *is* a vet of the histrionic TV docudrama, with appearances in ripped-from-the-headlines fare such as *Snowbound: The Jim and Jennifer Stolpa Story* (1994); *Woman Scorned: The Betty Broderick Story* (1992); *Switched at Birth* (1991). Other credits include the memorably weepy *Party of Five* "the drunk driver who killed our parents is out of jail" very special episode, as the drunk driver's remorseful daughter.

Lisa Gay Hamilton (**Rebecca Washington**): Plays the has-it-together woman who helps Donnell keep *The Practice* in practice. Has a previous Calista Flockhart connection: They both appeared in the downbeat 1995 drama, *Drunks*. Other

credits include *Beloved* (1998), *Jackie Brown* (1997) and *Twelve Monkeys* (1995).

*Other regulars of *The Practice* not featured on the *Ally* half of the crossover—Lara Flynn Boyle (Helen Gamble) and Michael Badalucco (Jimmy Berluti)—appeared with their fellow cast members on *The Practice* half, "Axe Murderer," also featuring Calista Flockhart (Ally McBeal) and Gil Bellows (Billy Thomas).

Part Three:
Episode Case Reviews

Chapter 13

The First Season (1997–98)

*This is the bottom line. When the pseudo-intellectual,
quasi-sociological debate mercifully subsides, all that
will matter is: Were the shows any good? Was* Ally
McBeal *good TV? Not important TV, not role-defin-
ing TV—just, was it good TV?*

*All right, so that's the question. And what fol-
lows is an answer. An answer based on a today's-eye
view of a contemporary show. Only Dionne Warwick's
psychic friends know for sure how* Ally *will play to
audiences of 2009 and beyond. Only they know if it'll
be a must-see Nick at Nite rerun. Or a three A.M. TV
Land museum piece. This is what we know—or, more
precisely, think—now.*

REGULAR CAST
Calista Flockhart (Ally McBeal)
Courtney Thorne-Smith (Georgia Thomas)
Greg Germann (Richard Fish)
Lisa Nicole Carson (Renee Radick)
Jane Krakowski (Elaine Vassal)

with Peter MacNicol* (John Cage)
and Gil Bellows (Billy Thomas)
Vonda Shepard (herself)
Regular cast status as of Episode 6

PRODUCTION/TECHNICAL CREDITS
Produced by David E. Kelley Productions, in association
    with 20th-Century Fox.

Creator: David E. Kelley
Executive producer: David E. Kelley
Co-executive producer: Jeffrey Kramer
Producers (various episodes): Mike Listo, Jonathan Pontell
Supervising producer: Jonathan Pontell
Co-producers: Steve Robin, Robert Breech, Pamela Wisne
Coordinating producers (various episodes): Gary M.
    Strangis, Peter Politanoff, Robert Breech
Director of photography: Billy Dickson
Main title theme and additional music: Vonda Shepard
Score: Danny Lux
Production designer (various episodes): Lee C. Fischer, Peter
    Politanoff
Editing (various episodes): Jonathan Pontell, Charles
    McClelland, Philip Neel, Thomas R. Moore, Bill
    Johnson
Casting: Jeanie Bacharach, Sharon Jetton
Original casting: Judith Weiner
Unit production manager: Robert Del Valle, Peter Burrell
First assistant director (various episodes): Allen DiGioia,
    Robert Vannetti

Second assistant director: Alisa Statman
Set decorator: Diane O'Connell
Set designer: Suzanne Feller-Otto
Lead person: David Lombard
Construction coordinator: John G. Heath Jr.
Property master: Douglas M. Keenan
Camera operator (various episodes): Michael Frediani,
    David Harp
Production sound mixer: Paul Lewis
Women's costume supervisor: Loree Parral
Men's costume supervisor: Shelly Levine
Key costumer: Michelle Roth
Location manager: Gary DeGalla
Gaffer: Myron Hyman
Key grip: J. David Ahuna
Choreography: Joe Malone
Transportation coordinator: Wayne Morris
Production accountant: Susan Stern
Production coordinator: Pam Jackson
Assistant production coordinator (various episodes): Jennifer
    Meyer, Evan Rabins
Head makeup artist: Joyce Westmore
Head hair stylist (various episodes): Ora Green, Robin
    Jacobs, Daphne Lawson, Gloria Ponce, Jeffrey Sacino,
    Lana Sharpe
Second second assistant director (various episodes): Scott
    Harris, Joel DeLoach
Assistant editor (various episodes): Jean Crupper, Michael
    Hathaway
Script supervisor: Mary C. Wright

Post-production supervisor: Kim Hamberg
Supervising sound editor: David Rawlinson
Re-recording mixers (various episodes): Harry Andronis,
     Thomas Gerard, Kurt Kassulke, Peter R. Kelsey, Nello
     Torri, Douglas E. Turner, David J. West
Music editor: Micdi Productions/Sharyn Tylk
Colorist: Dexter P.
Visual EFX supervisor (various episodes): Richard Kerrigan,
     Michael D. Most
Apprentice editor: Diane Holm
Post-production assistant: Noah Pontell
Production accountant: Susan Stern
Script coordinator: David Ransil
Production assistants: Leo Bauer, Kristin Means, Anne M.
     Uemura
Supervising associate: Roseann M. Bonora-Keris
Executive assistant: Cindy Lichtman
Associate to Jeffrey Kramer: Maggie Murphy
Assistant to Jeffrey Kramer: Mindy Farabee
Assistant to Jonathan Pontell: Cindy Kerber
Assistant to Mike Listo: Jennifer Menchaca
Assistant to Pamela Wisne (various episodes): Barb
     Mackintosh, Neely Swanson
Casting associate: Sharon Jetton
Filmed at: Ren-Mar Studios, Hollywood, California
Filmed with: Panavision (cameras and lenses)
Telecine, electronic assembly and visual effects supervision:
     Encore Video
Main title sequence created by: Imaginary Forces
Post-production sound editorial: West Productions Inc.

Dancing Baby provided courtesy of: Kinetix
Law books supplied by: West Publishing
Production accountants: Oberman, Tivioli & Miller, Ltd.
Location equipment: Cinelease, Inc.
Color: CFI Labs

RATING GUIDE: ☆☆☆☆ (very good); ☆☆☆ (good);
☆☆ (eh); ☆ (ick)

1. "Pilot"
Original air date: 9/8/97
Writer: David E. Kelley; director: James Frawley.

Guest cast: Larry Brandenburg (Judge Hopkins); Richard Riehle (Jack Billings); Pat McNamara (Ralph Lyne); David S. Dunard (Judge Hupp); Paul Collins (Judge Williams); Michael Mantell (Joseph Shapiro); Michael Caslin (Henry Thornton); Susan Knight (Joanne Wilder); Kim Delgado (Court Clerk); Jeffrey Kramer (Pedestrian); Tom Virtue (Ally's Father); Ashley Marie (Ally, ages 12–14); Michael Galeota (Billy, ages 12–14); Mike Boorem (Ally, age 7); Nicholas Pappone (Billy, age 7); Eric Cohen (Dancing Twin #1); Steve Cohen (Dancing Twin #2).

The brief: The starter—the one that maps out the history of Ally McBeal, twenty-seven-year-old Harvard–trained Boston lawyer, and Billy Thomas, The One True Love of Her Life (also a lawyer, and married—*not* to Ally.)

The verdict: ☆☆☆
Well-written, well-acted, blah, blah, blah . . . But come on, let's be honest. What makes this thing fly from the get-go is

that it plays like a really good *Three's Company*. Even better, it plays like the dirty-talking *Three's Company* that 1970s primetime standards never allowed it to be. And best yet, it plays like the *Three's Company* you can watch without shame because it features white-collar professionals instead of beach-bum roommates. Ally, Billy and Georgia, et al., use bigger (and better) words, but in their loins, they're Jack Tripper: dazed and confused and obsessed with sex.

If frisky Fox had existed as a TV network back in the 1970s, you can trust it would have been all over a property like *Three's Company*. But it didn't and it wasn't, so in the late 1990s it did the next best thing: it snapped up *Ally McBeal*—probably the second executives got to the part where Calista Flockhart's breasts make like inflatable beach balls. (The cries from the executive suite: "Whoo-hoo!")

Give David E. Kelley credit. He finally figured out how to make his penchant for the left-of-center play in the mainstream: Give 'em girls, girls, girls! (And don't forget the sex, sex, sex!) None of this makes Kelley's work insulting or demeaning to women. It makes it what it is: pleasant, often clever entertainment.

This episode scores points for being truly a fine first outing. TV pilots are tough things to fly—too many characters to introduce, too many character traits to hammer home. At its worst, *Ally*'s "Pilot" gets bogged down with too many daydream elements, too many Flockhart voice-overs, too many see-how-weird-we-can-be conceits. (Ally fell in love with Billy when she smelled his bottom?) But at its best? It's flat-out watchable.

Another random observation: Fashion police. So, the wardrobe department outfits Flockhart in the first round of what will become her trademark microskirts—and *then* they tie a muffler (all right, scarf) around her neck during the Big Courtroom Scene?!? What kind of fashion statement is that? You can't be Amanda Woodward *and* Rhoda Morgenstern.

Second opinion: "…Fast-paced, funny, touching, romantic and surprising. Please note that we did not add 'realistic.'"—*People.*

Background: A first, unaired version of "Pilot" featured actress Anna Gunn as Georgia. She appeared in only one scene (the "surprise, Billy has a wife" gag). When Thorne-Smith joined the cast, the entrance scene was reshot, plus Kelley gave Georgia a one-on-one showdown with Ally. Gunn licked her wounds over the Role That Got Away in a multiepisode guest stint on Kelley's other lawyer show, ABC-TV's *The Practice.*

Also cut from the trial-run "Pilot": a subplot involving an Ally ex-boyfriend, name of Steve.

He's billed as Glance Heavenward in the credits, but that's really series co-executive producer Jeffrey Kramer. He plays the poor sap who gets chewed out by Ally after bumping into her on the street. Kramer's no amateur thespian. He's a former actor with credits in everything from *Jaws* (1975) to *Santa Claus: The Movie* (1985).

The "You stinker!" thing explained: "You stinker!" is the cry uttered by the bowled-over granny in the end credit for Kelley's production company. The sequence is a nod to Kelley's grandmother, Mildred Kelley. The future TV mogul roomed with her during his first year of law school at Boston

The *Finder of Lost Loves* Connection

Cases are made here that *Ally McBeal* is, by turns, parts *thirtysomething*, *L.A. Law*, *Sisters*—with dashes of *Melrose Place* and *Three's Company*. But no discussion of *Ally* influences would be complete without a nod to a long-forgotten Aaron Spelling concoction, *Finder of Lost Loves*.

Said series appeared (briefly) on ABC during the 1984–85 season. It starred Tony Franciosa as a guy who essentially worked as a romance P.I. Much as *Ally*'s Cage/Fish and Associates specializes in sex-related litigation, Franciosa's TV firm (inexplicably, an ad agency) specialized in cases of the heart; if you needed to find a long-ago girlfriend or boyfriend, Cary Maxwell (Franciosa's character) was the man to see.

Being an Aaron Spelling production and not a David E. Kelley one, *Finder* was more convention than invention. (It was pretty much *Hotel* without the hotel or James Brolin.) But being an Aaron Spelling production, it also masterfully locked in on viewers' soft spots for sex, love and soap operas. The combo worked on *Fantasy Island*, it worked on *The Love Boat*, it worked on *Hotel* and, to a different degree, it works on *Ally*.

Why did *Finder* fail, where those shows succeeded? Bad time slot. Lousy ratings year for ABC. A briefly out-of-favor Spelling in his pre-*90210* revival phase. Also, it had one of TV's cheesiest-ever theme songs (warbled by Dionne Warwick, pre–Psychic Friends revival).

University. Kelley said he liked to try out his newfound legalese on Grandma. "She would go with it for a while and [then] she would say, 'You stinker.' Then it was over. She always got the last word," he told the *Los Angeles Daily News*. Still does.

Soundtrack notes: Shepard trots out her warmed-over, wannabe Carly Simon material—including "Neighborhood,"

"Maryland," "The Wildest Times of the World" and the inescapable theme song. She completes the mix with a 1960s cover tune, in this instance, "Tell Him." Kelley deploys said tunes during onscreen moments of Serious Contemplation. Fine, whatever. Every show (or, every *good* show) strives for a classy signature motif.

Here's the thing: *These songs* aren't *the right motif.* Not if they're about capturing the essence of a big-city, Generation X–era woman, anyway. On what planet do latter-day twenty-somethings groove, night in, and night out, to the *Mellow Sounds of the Seventies?* Well, on Planet *Ally,* to be sure. There, no one *ever* talks of R.E.M. or hears an old U2 song from high school in their heads or acknowledges they came of age in the New Wave 1980s. Of course not. There, people get misty-eyed nostalgic over stuff from *The Music Man* (?!?). Please. That Vonda Shepard's music *works* (and, sometimes, yes, it *is* effective) is evidence of *Ally McBeal*'s dirty little secret: A series ostensibly about young people is really a series about young people as refracted through the eyes of baby boomers. Now, *that's* the scandal *Time* magazine should be investigating.

2. "Compromising Positions"

Original air date: 9/15/97
Writer: David E. Kelley; director: Jonathan Pontell.

Guest cast: Peter MacNicol (John Cage); Dyan Cannon (Whipper Cone); Tate Donovan (Ronald Cheanie); Phil Leeds (Judge Boyle); Willie Garson (Frank Shea); John Cirigliano (Man #1); Robert Lee Jacobs (Greg Stone); Betty

Bridges-Nacasio (Clerk); Eric Cohen (Dancing Twin #1); Steve Cohen (Dancing Twin #2).

The brief: The one where we learn about our nutty new TV friends' quirks—the judge (Leeds) who inspects teeth, the law-firm partner (MacNicol) who takes "moments," the other law-firm partner (Germann) who, you know, fingers wattles.

The verdict: ☆☆☆
Actually, this should be considered the first in a *lengthy* series of episodes about the *Ally* people and their quirks. This one's more tolerable, and funny, than most because it was first. Also—and here's a biggie—this one's more tolerable, and funny, than most because the *Ally* people are still *people*. They're not the sum of their idiosyncrasies—yet. Oh, sure, we get the banter about "Fishisms" and "McBealisms" and "wattles" and "snappish" behavior, but all these future *Saturday Night Live*-esque catchphrases are uttered by characters who approximate human beings. Savor the hour.

Other random observations: How to tell a cut-above *Ally* episode from a cut-below *Ally* episode: (1) Flockhart's hair is approximately chin-length, (2) Dyan Cannon guest-stars. (Her Whipper is the series' good-luck charm. She descales Fish.)

Three's Company Watch: this episode's Jack Tripper moment: Billy thinks Ally is going to tell Georgia he had sex with a bachelor-party call girl, except at the last second Ally concocts a kooky alternative explanation . . . which makes everybody happy! (Janet saves Jack's bacon again!)

Background: MacNicol gets "special appearance" billing here. Bit player Betty Bridges-Nacasio is the mother of Todd (*Diff'rent Strokes*) Bridges, who, in his day, could have run up a tidy defendant's bill at Cage/Fish.

According to the *Webster's New World Dictionary*, a wattle is a "fleshy flap of skin hanging from the throat of certain birds or lizards." Just a guess, but we're betting that's not the way they described the bit to Dyan Cannon.

Veteran character actor Phil Leeds died on August 16, 1998, at age eighty-two. This was his first of five *Ally* appearances.

Soundtrack notes: A hint of *Leave It to Beaver*, a touch of Vonda (at the very, very end). Lots of voice-over, apparently not a lot of room for music.

3. "The Kiss"

Original air date: 9/22/97
Writer: David E. Kelley; director: Dennie Gordon.

Guest cast: Kate Jackson (Barbara Cooker); Tate Donovan (Ronald Cheanie); Richard Riehle (Jack Billings); David Spielberg (Cooker's Ex-boss); Alaina Reed Hall (Judge Witt); Nelson Mashita (Foreperson); Cissy Wellman (Secretary).

The brief: The one about the deposed TV anchor (Jackson) who pursues an age-discrimination suit against her old station.

The verdict: ☆☆☆
Jackson's great, the courtroom stuff's fun—all in all, pretty airtight. That is, if you forgive the awkward/convenient

device of Georgia swooping in out of nowhere and inviting Ally to help argue Cooker's case. Likely? Hey, all's fair in upping the dramatic ante of a love triangle. And, besides, imagine, if you will, the op-ed pieces if Kelley had dared to write Ally and Georgia as catfighting adversaries instead of professionally peaceable colleagues.

Other random observations: Win one, lose one—Bellows ditches the dorky little Caesar bangs he sported in the first two episodes; Thorne-Smith *doesn't* ditch her *Melrose Place* do—which is only about a hundred times more *un*lawyerlike than Flockhart's skirts.

Dump it: So, when Ally thinks she's about to get dumped by sort-of love-interest Ronald Cheanie, she pictures a (get this?) Dumpster. Clever, right? Well, uh, no.

Second opinion: In a piece for the *Village Voice*, critic Tom Carson contended that the episode's opening scene—Flockhart trying on a pair of jeans on her desk, while Krakowski observes from ground level—was a "lesbian sight gag."

(Unsolicited second opinion to the second opinion: You know, people, sometimes TV is just TV.)

Background: That was no random dig at *Entertainment Weekly* in one of Ally's courtroom voice-overs (the one where she equates the magazine's vast readership with proof of America's vast capacity for stupidity). According to *Daily Variety*, it was Kelley's payback for an *EW* writer he felt backstabbed the show in print following a visit to the set.

Kate Jackson is best known for her 1976–79 TV run as Sabrina Duncan, aka the Smart Angel, on *Charlie's Angels*.

Alaina Reed Hall is best known for her 1985–90 TV run on *227*, aka the Dumb Marla Gibbs Sitcom.

Soundtrack notes: Lots of Vonda nightclub action. (Those supposedly sharp lawyers just eat up that T.G.I.Friday's vibe, don't they?)

Major play here for one of the series' recurring themes: "It's in His Kiss (The Shoop Shoop Song)." Fine. Whatever. There's nothing inherently wrong with the tune—unless you remember it also was used as a major plot point on a very special episode of *Growing Pains*. *Ally*, like life, is best enjoyed when you're not thinking of Kirk Cameron.

4. "The Affair"

Original air date: 9/29/97
Writer: David E. Kelley; director: Arlene Sanford.

Guest cast: Kathy Baker (Katherine Dawson); Brett Cullen (James Dawson); Tate Donovan (Ronald Cheanie); Jerry Hardin (Priest); Jenjer Vick (Secretary); Alexis Kleyla (Cara Dawson, age 8); Holliston Coleman (Cara Dawson, age 4),

The brief: The one about the dead professor (Cullen) with whom Ally had an affair (while he was alive).

The verdict: ☆☆☆
Angst, poignancy and Kelley's dedication to writing a character who is decidedly *not* perfect (sometimes not even admirable) make this a stand-out. Flockhart's best Mary Tyler Moore–style flummox through a eulogy monologue doesn't hurt, either. Neither does a nifty bit where nothing

but a series of looks tells the professor's widow (Baker) all she needs to know about the true nature of Ally's relationship with her husband.

But beware. The good merely serves to obscure the gathering storm clouds: The nonsense about Elaine's face bra; the over-the-top foot-in-mouth special effect and the reference to Billy being the kind of guy who reads *Men Are from Mars, Women Are from Venus*. (Please. Is there *any* kind of guy who reads that stuff?) All the signs are there. This is a show primed for a descent into Quirky City.

Background: Kathy Baker starred as Dr. Jill Brock in Kelley's *Picket Fences* (1992–96). She also appeared in his 1996–penned feature film, *To Gillian on Her 37th Birthday*.

Brett Cullen has appeared in one bajillion (rough estimate) TV shows and movies. His most recent: the UPN series *Legacy* (1998–). His most notable: a 1986–88 stint on prime-time soap *Falcon Crest*.

Soundtrack notes: Billy and Ally slowdance to "You Belong to Me"—because even though, you know, they allegedly grew up in the age of John Hughes movies, it's *The Big Chill* that apparently molded their musical tastes. (Yeesh.)

Vonda moves out from behind the piano to prove to TV audiences that she does too have legs.

5. "One Hundred Tears Away"
Original air date: 10/20/97
Writer: David E. Kelley; director: Sandy Smolan.

Guest cast: Dyan Cannon (Whipper Cone); Zeljko Ivanek (Board of Overseers Judge); Phil Leeds (Judge Boyle); Keene Curtis (Judge Hawk); Carol Locatell (Board of Overseers Judge); Audrie Neenan (Mrs. Clarkson); Betty Bridges-Nacasio (Clerk); Daniel Hutchinson (Officer Kenter); Gerald Emerick (Johnson); Eric Cohen (Dancing Twin #1); Steve Cohen (Dancing Twin #2).

The brief: The one about the can of Pringles.

The verdict: ☆☆☆☆

This is how fast things move in the superinformation age. A mere six weeks after its premiere, Kelley is already cranking out a script that responds to his critics and gives 'em what they want to see: Ally McBeal put on trial for being annoying, petulant Ally McBeal.

The inciting incident is one that'll likely get "clipped" on Emmy nights of the future: Ally tripping a woman over a can of Pringles. With their lead oddball facing suspension from the bar, the *Ally* players momentarily abandon their own private, oddball worlds and argue Kelley's seasonlong thesis (one of them, anyway): There's nothing wrong with being different. And they're right—there is nothing wrong with being different. So long as "being different" isn't your sole reason for being. (A trap that later snares the series.)

In any case, good stuff. Quintessential *Ally*, quintessentially good TV—down to the line about how Ally wouldn't want to be homeless because then she wouldn't get to wear her "outfits." The line eventually would be read back to Kelley as further proof that he aimed to trivialize women in general,

and women lawyers in particular. Absurd. The line is further proof that sometimes Kelley can *just nail it*. Vanity-free, "any old robe will do" Mother Teresa was the exception; the Allys of the working world are the rule—they drag themselves to their offices each morning to show the world their "outfits." Nothing wrong with that, either.

Second opinion: " . . . How smart for Kelley to devise a script that forces [Ally] and all who love her to answer to [the character's] excesses."—*USA Today*

Background: The final scene—Ally phoning her parents after a tough week—hit home for Flockhart's real-life parents. "I'll have to admit, I had a tear in my eye when she said, 'Goodbye Dad,'" dad Ronald Flockhart said to the *Tribune* of Morristown, Tennessee.

Jeffrey Kramer (unbilled this time—nary even a nod as Glance Heavenward) pops up again to provide evidence of the street-bumping incident.

Phil Leeds makes his second appearance—and second partially clothed one at that. Once was enough on the latter count.

What a small, global world: Croat-born Zeljko Ivanek played Bobby Kennedy in HBO's *The Rat Pack* (1998).

Ally makes history as the first primetime show to link Omar Sharif (*Doctor Zhivago*) and contraceptive jelly in the same expressed thought.

Soundtrack notes: Good thing the show keeps Vonda on retainer. All those shots of people (usually Flockhart) walking and keeping counsel with their thoughts on lonesome, rain-

slicked streets would seem lonesome without *something* going on in the background. Suffice to say there's lots of walking-and-thinking scenes in this one. And, in turn, tons o' Vonda ("Neighborhood").

There's also a lot of nightclub stuff. Including a bit (a reference to the overt use of "Don't Walk Away Renee") where the characters acknowledge that they *do* hear what Vonda plays. So much for the deaf defense.

6. "The Promise"

Original air date: 10/27/97
Writer: David E. Kelley; director: Victoria Hochberg.

Guest cast: Jay Leggett (Harry Pippen); Rusty Schwimmer (Angela Tharpe); Jamie Rose (Sandra Winchell); Michael Winters (Judge Spitt); Michael Bofshever (Judge Stephenson) James Mathers (Dr. Carpenter); Brooke Burns (The Girl, Jennifer Higgin).

The brief: The one about the fat attorney (Leggett) whom Ally saves with CPR.

The verdict: ☆☆
A step back—and a step back that coincides, not at all coincidentally, with the emergence of Peter MacNicol as a full-fledged staff member (albeit, one not yet featured in the opening credits). This is not a knock on MacNicol—he's wonderful. Really. He's got presence, he's got intelligence—he's got a script that tells him to be too damned precious. On another series (or, better, in a Tennessee Williams play),

Unisex Bathrooms: Flush Right with the Future?

It was the breakout gimmick of *Ally McBeal's* first season: the unisex. David E. Kelley told *TV Guide* the idea was to give his characters a "unique" meeting ground. Or as a male thirtysomething Manhattan private investigator who has toiled in an office with a single-toilet unisex bathroom, delicately puts it: "The dynamic of the show is that men and women are in there [um, experiencing the dividends of a fiber-rich diet] at the same time." Indeed.

But does what makes for good drama (or comedy) on TV, make for good man-woman relationships (not to mention, hygiene) in real life? Well, to be sure, the unisex is hardly an untested concept. All but the most fortunate cope with cramped unisexes every day in our homes and apartments. It's called The Curse of Only One Bathroom. Small businesses, like the aforementioned PI's firm, similarly rely on single-stall unisexes to serve *all* its employees' primping and relieving needs. Does the concept work? Functionally, yes. Is it always pretty? No. Oh, well. Such are the indignities of underfunded plumbing facilities.

What makes the Kelley vision of the unisex different, of course, is that men and women not only share the same pipes, they share them *at the same time*.

"There's no privacy *anywhere*," recurring guest star Dyan Cannon (Whipper Cone) said, in *Entertainment Weekly*. "You can get in a lot of trouble in that bathroom."

Ah, but a *cool* kind of trouble. On *Ally*, the unisex is the adult stand-in for the high-school locker hall—the sexually charged place where boys and girls hang, gossip and goof off before homeroom and/or court. All in all, kind of an appealing notion.

Craig Yarde, of Yarde Metals in Connecticut, told ABCNews.com that his metal-distributing firm planned to install a unisex at its new facility—a move

inspired in part by *Ally*. What started out as a joke, Yarde told the news service, ended up making business sense. "[W]e think it does send a message to all our associates that we're all in it together," he said.

Well, it's a nice thought, anyway: Higher consciousness and/or greater understanding through unisex bathrooms. There's at least some symbolic truth to the concept—the breaking of barriers, the demystification of the genders, the feeling that, as Yarde put it, "we're all in it together."

In reality, it's doubtful *Ally* is going to establish the unisex as the bathroom standard in the United States. Not as long as there are babies that need to be changed. Or feminine-hygiene vending machines (conveniently absent on *Ally*) that need to be restocked.

The truth is, *Ally* omits the nitty-gritty of office bathroom maintenance (not that we're complaining). On the series, the unisex works because the most unpleasant thing the characters have to put up with is the odd isometric dismount by Peter MacNicol's John Cage. There are no frank arguments about who did or didn't put down a seat, who did or didn't clean up after themselves, who did or didn't plug up a toilet.

Again, that's fine for the TV show. But in the real world? Boys will be boys; girls will be girls. In separate rooms, please.

MacNicol's Cage would bring a welcome sense of daft. On *Ally*, he's but the latest loon. In fact, he's *the biggest loon*. Remember how last episode's message was, Being Different is Okay? Turned out it wasn't a defense of the Ally character at all—it was an excuse to foist a slow-water-pouring, moment-taking, nose-whistling *freak* on the viewing public. Enough.

To be fair, this episode has more problems than Cage. For one thing, it's got a big "who cares?" subplot involving Ally, the fat attorney and his fiancée (Schwimmer). And for another thing, it's already repeating itself: Yet *another* solicita-

tion case? Is Cage/Fish located in the red-light district of Boston?

Background: Brooke Burns makes her first of three appearances here as the delivery girl who gives the show's special-effects whizzes all sorts of opportunity to graft giant, drooping tongues onto the faces of her male costars. In 1998, Burns fulfilled her destiny, joining the cast of bathing-suit drama *Baywatch*.

Falcon Crest Watch: Jamie Rose is yet another alum of the Jane Wyman soap. She costarred as willful daughter (is there any other kind on soaps?) Victoria Gioberti from 1981–83. She's also a David Kelley alum, with a recurring stint on *Chicago Hope* during the 1994–95 season.

Eagle-eyed Kelley fans will recall Rusty Schwimmer from the 1992 pilot of *Picket Fences*. (She appeared in that episode with future Janet Reno imitator, Linda Gehringer.)

Jay Leggett appeared on Fox's *In Living Color* from 1993–94.

Soundtrack notes: The *Music Man* episode. Flockhart and Carson warble "Goodnight, My Someone." Do today's twentysomethings really get teary-eyed over Meredith Wilson? Well, no doubt, some do. But as for the real-world chances of two twentysomething roommates (non–Broadway gypsies, both) sharing the same instant recall of Meredith Wilson? Suffice to say, the selection doesn't score the show a lot of points in the credibility department.

On the upside, of course, a reality-challenged moment like this helps keeps things in perspective. Namely: It's a TV show, not a documentary.

Walking-and-Thinking Scene Watch: Ally (natch), with a Vonda-rendered version of "True Love."

7. "The Attitude"

Original air date: 11/3/97
Writer: David E. Kelley; director: Michael Schultz.

Guest cast: Brenda Vaccaro (Karen Horowitz); Steve Vinovich (Jerry Burrows); Jason Blicker (Rabbi Stern); Andrew Heckler (D.A. Jason Roberts); Eric Cohen (Dancing Twin #1); Steve Cohen (Dancing Twin #2).

The brief: The one about (*a*) the rabbi (Blicker), (*b*) the guy (Heckler) with salad dressing on his face and (*c*) Georgia's lawsuit. And, yeah, these disparate points hang together about as poorly as can be expected.

The verdict: ☆

For the record, let it be stated that Kelley's Ally has a right to say anything that comes out of her mouth. There is no grounds for the argument, "Oh, but Ally would *never* say that." Bull. Ally is *not* a real person—she can say anything Kelley thinks is funny and/or dramatic. That said, let the record further state that Ally would *never* say some of the stuff Kelley sticks her with here. Mixing up "mistletoe" for "mazel tov" is funny *if the character is ten years old*—and not a Harvard-trained lawyer. That's how lame some of the comedy is. And that's how lame the story line with Ally, the rabbi and the woman (Vaccaro) who wants the rabbi's permission to remarry in his synagogue, is. There's no real dramatic stakes (the main stumbling block is resolved far too easily). There's no real connection to the Georgia story line (or the thing about the date with the salad-dressing guy). There are just excuses for Ally to call a yarmulke a "beanie."

Not that the Georgia story line (she sues her firm) is a big winner, either. It's just an excuse to better integrate Thorne-Smith (barely around for the last two episodes) into the show and better integrate Georgia into Cage/Fish— right down to the shared-stall bathroom moment with Ally. (Ha! . . . *Not*.)

No one escapes with dignity intact. Krakowski slips into zany, kooky, weird gear—bypassing the "just human" off-ramp entirely. MacNicol pops up on the (what else?) bagpipes.

Attention ladies and gentlemen: Show overboard! Show overboard!

Background: Don't worry about Brenda Vaccaro. She survived *Airport '77*—she can survive this thing.

MacNicol really *does* play the bagpipes.

Soundtrack notes: Outside of the cool cover of Herb Alpert's "This Guy's in Love with You," the music here is just as stinky—in an appropriate sort of way. How better to end an episode all too in love with its nuttiness, than to have the characters gather for a celebratory dance set to the show's own theme song? Perfect. In a perfectly awful sort of way.

8. "Drawing the Lines"

Original air date: 11/10/97

Writer: David E. Kelley; director: Mel Damski.

Guest cast: Sandra Bernhard (Caroline Poop); Cristine Rose (Marci Hatfield); Stan Ivar (Jason Hatfield); Mark Metcalf

(Jason Hatfield's lawyer); Brooke Burns (The Girl, Jennifer Higgin).

The brief: The how-to-drink-cappuccino episode.

The verdict: ☆☆

Getting back on track. The opening scene—Ally instructing Georgia on the finer points of cappuccino drinking—scores big snicker points for prompting a broadcast network to air a close-up of a woman licking semen, er, milk froth from her lips. How HBO. Jack Tripper would be proud. Among, um, other things. (Imagine, on *Three's Company*, they couldn't even get the word "toilet" past the censors!)

Now for the not-so good stuff: Cage and the nose-whistling; Krakowski's Elaine and everything. They're both annoying, and—as the novelty of their madness wears thin—ho-hum, a deadly combo.

All this, plus—plus!—a phoned-in performance by per-formance artist Sandra Bernhard as an attorney handling Elaine's would-be legal attempt to make the guys stop ogling Brooke Burns.

One more thing: This is but the eighth—*eighth!*—episode, yet it feels like the millionth time a story concludes on a shot of Flockhart (what else?) walking and thinking. Once, it's evocative. Twice, it's a theme. More, it's a *cliché*—as corny as a soap opera relying on an extreme close-up of a diva's trembling lip to segue into the next Huggies commercial.

Background: Sandra Bernhard said initially she wasn't thrilled about Kelley's offer to play Poop. "I can't really jump

up and down about playing a lawyer," she told the *New York Post*. Really? We couldn't tell.

This episode was rated TV-14 D, meaning it contains dialogue with sexual innuendo and isn't considered suitable for kids under fourteen—even though you'd guess that thirteen-year-old boys would get the biggest kick out the cappuccino scene.

Soundtrack notes: You knew it was only a matter of time before the supreme self-pitying baby-boomer anthem "It's My Party" turned up on this closet boomer show. And you were right.

9. "The Dirty Joke"
Original air date: 11/17/97
Writer: David E. Kelley; director: Daniel Attias.

Guest cast: Sandra Bernhard (Caroline Poop); Keene Curtis (Judge Hawk); Brooke Burns (The Girl, Jennifer Higgin); Nate Reese (Clerk); Eric Cohen (Dancing Twin #1); Steve Cohen (Dancing Twin #2).

The brief: The one about Ally and Renee's dirty-joke contest.

The verdict: ☆☆☆
Everything an *Ally* episode should be. Funny, semi-real and decidedly low on the see-how-clever-we-are scale (save for a quick Barbara Walters fantasy gag). Kelley doesn't need tricks when he's got the goods—and he's got the goods in Flockhart and Carson, and a pair of absolutely winning performances. Flockhart's turn is appreciated, but almost expected by this

point. Carson's is the revelation. She finally gets to strut after being cooped up on the sidelines. Here, her bawdy Renee literally saunters into the spotlight. About time.

The episode feeds off Carson's frisky vibe. There's a rare primetime utterance of "Bite me." There's a tasteless joke about an armless, legless woman. There's an off-color joke about two fleas and oral sex. And for a welcome change, there's a twist on the inevitable walking-and-thinking shot (Flockhart does a *happy* walk-and-think thing). In short, the episode's got a pulse.

Other random observations: The Cage factor—there's none. MacNicol is MIA. Suspiciously, the show's a lot better. Hmm.

Lose the lisp: Flockhart can do many things very well—a decent Barbara Walters impression is not one of them.

Second time's the charm: Sandra Bernhard rebounds with a lifelike performance.

A theory of *Ally*'s success: For the second episode in a row, Flockhart pretends to eat Ben & Jerry's ice cream (what she's doing is called *stirring*, not *eating*) while lounging in a pair of pajamas. Stuff like that is gold. There are few more alluring images to the modern-day city dweller than this idyllic picture of consumer comfort—of curling up in flannel, watching TV, noshing on ice cream *and* (despite all these couch-potato tendencies) looking like a stick figure. It's the way people live in Blockbuster commercials and Land's End catalogs. And it's the way we want to live, too, dammit.

Second opinion: " . . . Not since Frasier read Dickens to the barflies at *Cheers* while the jilted Rebecca did a Miss

Havisham have I enjoyed a sitcom as much."—author Olivia Goldsmith (*The First Wives Club*), in an essay for the *New York Times*

Background: There are lots of references to the rabbi from "The Attitude" here, and with good reason: the rabbi character was supposed to be back. He was even supposed to be in the crowd when Ally bombs with her flea joke. But, alas, the cutting-room floor claims the best of 'em.

That's the 1962 Bette Davis–Joan Crawford camp classic, *What Ever Happened to Baby Jane?* on the tube in the opening scene.

Brooke Burns speaks! After two episodes of being worshipped from afar, she gets actual lines when her character threatens to sue Cage/Fish. Once she opens her mouth, though, the spell apparently is broken. She never shows up on *Ally* again.

This episode was branded TV-14 DL for offensive, as well as sexually tinged, dialogue.

Soundtrack notes: Vonda speaks—twice! And, in a surreal TV moment, she's introduced to the adoring bar crowd as Vonda Shepard. So, what's the deal? Is she supposed to be playing someone who looks and sounds like Vonda? Is she supposed to be playing herself? And if she's supposed to be real, what does that say about the other (*wink-wink*) "characters"? The mind reels.

In another welcome change, there's a nice mix of songs: "My Favorite Things" (from *Sound of Music*); "The Way You Do the Things You Do"; and the knee-jerk (given the nature of the episode) "I Started a Joke."

10. "Boy to the World"

Original air date: 12/1/97
Writer: David E. Kelley; director: Thomas Schlamme.

Guest cast: Dyan Cannon (Whipper Cone); Wilson Cruz (Stephanie/Steven Grant); Amy Aquino (Dr. Harper); Armin Shimerman (Judge Walworth); Harrison Page (Reverend Newman); Jennifer Holliday (Choir Soloist); Ronald Hunter (Detective Greene); Daniel Wantland (D.A. Corbett); Niles Brewster (Attorney Ken Banks).

The brief: The one about the (*a*) transvestite (Cruz), and (*b*) the "Short People" funeral service.

The verdict: ☆☆☆☆☆

The stand-out of Season No. 1. A flat-out miracle of an episode; why, Ally McBeal seems almost adultlike.

Now, Kelley has every right to write his characters as silly as he wants. But when he chooses to write the Cage/Fish lawyers like he does here, they're really something. They're human.

The biggest special effect deployed here is emotion— Ally and the increasingly irrelevant Elaine coming to the aid of the young transvestite (an outstanding Cruz); Cage getting too caught up in an attraction to Ally to get goofy; Fish being humanized by the death of his short people–hating uncle.

So, this is what these characters are like underneath all the flip "bygones" crap? Nice to meet them.

If nothing else (and there's lots to recommend here), this episode is significant for a single shot of Flockhart. The scene: the church memorial service. The setup: Jennifer

Holliday belting "Short People," the *Ally* cast smirking and shifting in their seats for a series of reaction shots. And then: Flockhart. Her face: screwed up in this defiant/pouty/determined/bemused expression. How do you get all that stuff in a single two-second take? Flockhart is doing stuff that's not on the page. She is doing stuff that keeps this show watchable even when it's not all that.

One downside: Cruz gets killed off. Too bad—the show could have used him.

Other random observations: Oh, that David Kelley. "Humping." Can you say "humping" on primetime? On a Christmas episode? Guess so.

The Whipper Factor: Dyan Cannon is back. Suspiciously, the show is *much* better. Hmm.

Second opinion: " . . . This is one episode not to miss."—*New York Daily News*

Background: Wilson Cruz cut his heels as the transvestite Angel in the Broadway and Los Angeles productions of *Rent*. He's best known to TV audiences as Rickie Vasquez on *My So-Called Life* (1994–95).

Director Thomas Schlamme's Kelley connection goes back to gigs on *Chicago Hope* and *The Practice* and extends to his marriage to *Chicago Hope* star Christine Lahti.

If you don't recognize Armin Shimerman, that's because he's usually buried under makeup as alien Quark on *Star Trek: Deep Space Nine*.

If you don't recognize Jennifer Holliday, that's because the *Dreamgirls* Tony winner used to be 180 pounds heavier.

"When I told [the *Ally* producers] I had lost the weight, they had to think about hiring me," she told the *New York Post.* "But in the end, David and the other producers were very happy." Guess so. She returned for more screen time in Season No. 2.

Soundtrack notes: Vonda croons the usual holiday suspects— "Jingle Bell Rock" and "Let It Snow," plus offers a nifty snippet of "The Chipmunk Song (Christmas Don't Be Late)"—rendering that whiny Alvin, Simon and Theodore tune almost, you know, heartbreaking. The miracle of Christmas works in strange ways.

11. "Silver Bells"

Original air date: 12/15/97
Writer: David E. Kelley; director: Joe Napolitans.

Guest cast: Dyan Cannon (Whipper Cone); Eric Pierpoint (James Horton); Katie Mitchell (Pattie Horton); Amanda Carlin (Mindy Horton); Renee Goldsberry (Ikette #1); Vatrena King (Ikette #2); Sy Smith (Ikette #3); Peter Roth (Network President); Bailey Thompson (Jean Horton); Eric Cohen (Dancing Twin #1); Steve Cohen (Dancing Twin #2).

The brief: The *other* Christmas episode—the one with the (*a*) office party, and (*b*) the threesome (Pierpoint, Mitchell and Carlin) who go to court to become a *legally married* threesome.

The verdict: ☆☆☆
You gotta love a show that does not one—but *two*— Christmas episodes. And, for your own personal safety, you

gotta love a show that's a fan favorite. This is one of those foolproof, people-pleasin' Very Special Episodes—even if it doesn't really make any sense. Honestly, this installment—featuring stage performances by Carson, Germann and Krakowski—plays like an old episode of *Alice*, one where the gang at Mel's volunteers to produce a variety show for a local rest home: Suddenly, characters who displayed no known talents outside of slinging hash and eking out a minimum-wage existence, are hoofing and singing like the seasoned stage vets that the actors who portray them are. This is all entertaining, of course, but it loses sight of the big picture: If Vera really had an employable talent, would she *really* sublimate it in order to live out her days in a hellhole restaurant in the middle of the Arizona desert? Please. The same can be asked of the apparently showbiz-ready *Ally* gang—particularly Carson's Renee. That woman belongs on a stage with Liza, not in a courtroom.

Other random observations: It never fails—Dyan Cannon: good episode. Natch. (If only someone would send her on a mercy mission to *Suddenly Susan*, or something.)

Unexplained mystery of the universe: Long blonde hair makes woman-of-a-certain-age Cannon look contemporary; long blonde hair makes barely-thirty Thorne-Smith look dated.

Background: Eric Pierpoint is best known for looking like a potato-head in the sci-fi cop drama *Alien Nation* (1989–90, plus subsequent TV movies).

The guy who brags he's a network president at the Christmas-party scene *really* was a network president. That's former Fox honcho Peter Roth.

Soundtrack verdict: This is what makes this one fun—Krakowski's "I Saw Mommy Kissing Santa Claus" (with the Ikettes), Germann's "I Love You More Today Than Yesterday" and Carson and Vonda's duet, "Santa Claus Is Coming to Town."

12. "Cro-Magnon"

Original air date: 1/4/98
Writer: David E. Kelley; director: Allan Arkush.

Guest cast: Michael Easton (Glenn); Lee Wilkof (D.A.); Michael Winters (Judge Spitt); Henry Woronicz (Austin Gill); Eddie Mills (Clinton Gill); Derk Cheetwood (Dwayne Stokes); Nicolette Vajtay (Jill); Sharon Omni (Bailiff); Karen Elyse (Foreperson); Barry Livingston (Dr. Emburg); Dancing Baby (his own creepy self).

The brief: The one about (*a*) the big penis, and (*b*) the Dancing Baby.

The verdict: ☆☆☆
This isn't the finest *Ally*, but it is, perhaps, the time-capsule *Ally*. You want to explain to future viewers what all the hype, all the magazine covers, were about? You show them this.

First, you get a story line about a nude model (Easton) with a huge penis. Second, you get a story line about an imaginary baby (Dancing Baby). Sex and babies and *Big Chill* music (the DB's "Hooked on a Feeling" theme). On second thought, this episode isn't quintessential *Ally*, it's quintessential Americana.

All this sizzle masks a larger problem, though: Kelley's Ally is slipping into insanity. The Pringles incident was out there, but still well within the realm of "normal" human behavior. The Dancing Baby is a hallucination of *Twilight Zone* proportions. Sure, the gag's cute. And, sure, it's even cuter when Flockhart bops around in her jammies with the creepy little thing. But, in the long run, this is *not* a good thing.

Consider the lesson of *Sisters*. *Sisters* (1991–96) was a *thirtysomething* wannabe with a twist: The show employed two sets of sisters—one all-adult, the other all-kid. Every episode, the adults vividly remembered something about their childhoods—to the point where they'd stop and *relive* the moment as kids. At first, the device was, yes, kind of cute. Then it got kind of weird—to the point where the audience was left to ask, What *were* these people smoking? To wit: You don't have to identify with a character, but you have to believe that the character *might* be able to identify with you, Joe or Jane Human.

Another random observation: Knockout: A nifty piece of writing and editing—crosscutting Ally and the penis guy's roll on the living-room floor with a boxing match.

Background: This was the highest-rated *Ally* to date— watched in just under nine million TV homes. Size *does* matter.

Gil Bellows on the size issue, in *TV Guide*: "Women have shared their philosophies and preferences with me. . . . [And his take?] Everything matters."

This episode sparked a run on Nick and Nora pajamas— the daffy designer duds modeled by Flockhart in the big

Dancing Baby scene. Women's costume supervisor Loree Parral told *People* that Flockhart felt an immediate kinship to the PJs: "She said, 'Oh, my gosh, I just got a pair of these for my birthday. I love them.'"

Peter MacNicol finally makes the opening credits, effective this outing.

Barry Livingston played Ernie Douglas (the kid with the glasses) on *My Three Sons* from 1965 to 1972.

Soundtrack notes: What can you say about an episode where the Dancing Baby's "ooga-chaka" chant is the defining musical moment? Not much. Other than, Thank God every episode is only about forty-five minutes, minus commercials.

A much better moment comes when Flockhart and Easton plunk out "Heart and Soul" on the piano.

13. "The Blame Game"
Original air date: 1/19/98
Writer: David E. Kelley; director: Sandy Smolan.

Guest cast: Michael Easton (Glenn); Harry J. Lennix (Ballard); Elizabeth Ruscio (Cynthia Pierce); Ben Siegler (Hoverless); Adrian Sparks (Katz); Susan Merson (Judge Stoller); Daniel Mahar (Michael Lamb); Dale Weston (Reporter); Vince Brocato (Foreperson); Dean Purvis (Man); Renee Goldsberry, Vatrena King and Sy Smith (The Ikettes); Christopher Michael (Bailiff); Dancing Baby (His own creepy self).

The brief: The "penguin" episode.

The verdict: ☆☆
The anticlimax to last episode's hot-and-heavy panting. Oh, Ally and the penis guy have sex again—but we're told, not shown, this. In this case, discretion is the better part of female bonding—the real point of the episode. Ally, Renee and Georgia team to pay back penis guy for "tricking" Ally into having sex with him. The plan they hatch allows Kelley to introduce yet another catchphrase to mainstream America: "the penguin," aka a "pantsing." Overall, a big "eh." Not great, not awful. Nothing special.

Other random observations: Oh, that David Kelley, Part I: He virtually slips in a not-ready-for-primetime cuss word, writing a bit where Ally rcfcrs to Billy as "ass holy."

Oh, that David Kelley, Part II: A pissy, jealous Billy calls Ally a "bitch." Nothing shocking. Not by modern-day *Melrose Place* standards, anyway. But, still, a little harsh for a series where the characters are about as edgy as gumdrops.

Second opinion: *Us* magazine takes exception to the scene where Ally offers simultaneous apologies to the penis guy and Billy: "Whose three-way fantasy is that?!"

Second opinion to the second opinion: Sometimes an apology is just an apology.

Background: *Entertainment Weekly* spotted this one first. In the courtroom subplot, Ally and Cage pursue a judgment against an airline for the mysterious crash of a "flight 111"—the same flight number of the real-life doomed Swiss Air jet that mysteriously crashed in September 1998, killing all onboard.

Soundtrack notes: Nice use of "Na, Na, Hey, Hey, Kiss Him Good-bye" (better known as the fan-participation "na-na-na-na" taunt in ballparks the nation over) in the scene where penis guy dumps Ally in the bar. One of the series' best marriages of music and story line yet.

14. "Body Language"

Original air date: 2/2/98

Writers: David E. Kelley, Nicole Yorkin and Dawn Prestwich; director: Mel Damski.

Guest cast: Dyan Cannon (Whipper Cone); Kathleen Wilhoite (Janie Bittner); Lawrence Pressman (Judge Smart); J. Kenneth Campbell (Donald Yorkin); John Thaddeus (Michael Young); Linda Gehringer (Janet Reno); David Doty (Minister); Jeffrey von Meyer (Attorney Skroot); Carrie Stauber (Female Cop); Evan O'Meara (Male Cop); Bill Dwyer (Bandleader); Annika Brindley (Tory); Eric Mansker (Bailiff); Nancy Stephens (Dr. Karp); Eric Cohen (Dancing Twin #1); Steve Cohen (Dancing Twin #2).

The brief: The one about the Fish fingering Janet Reno's wattle.

The verdict: ☆☆

Not even Dyan Cannon can (totally) save this one. What starts out as promising—an almost operatic battle for a bridal bouquet between perennial bridesmaids Ally and Renee—ends up contrived—an unspeakably stupid sequence wherein Ally dances in the snow in her new Nick and Noras for all of her adoring friends to see. Please. Anybody know when the

The Janet Reno Thing

What is it that bewitches us so about the United States Attorney General? What is it that inspires David E. Kelley to write the woman as the object of Richard Fish's desire?

Perhaps the same thing that, according to the *Weekly World News*, made her the top choice in a 1997 poll that asked Japanese men what woman they would most want to be stranded with on an island.

All right, granted, yes, it's the *Weekly World News* we're talking about here. Bat Boy probably came in a close second.

And yet . . . The thing that makes the *Weekly World News* story so funny, the thing that makes Kelley's Fish-Reno stuff so electric, is that there *is* something intriguing about our nation's top crime-fighter.

Oh, Janet Reno, how do we count the ways?

The hair: It's been derided as a mop. It's been put down as bed-head. But Reno faithfuls know better. It's a tribute to 1964–era Mick Jagger. And it works. How silly would Janet Reno look in a perm or a fussy do? But the bangs-and-bob look? Perfect. It says, "I'm busy." It says, "I'm substance over image." It says, "(I Can't Get No) Satisfaction."

The glasses: They don't make 'em like that anymore. Specs are virtually unisex now. One slim, squared-off style fits all. But that doesn't cut it with Reno. She's a woman who favors old-school, plastic-framed, Jackie O–era girlie glasses. Hear her roar.

The size: Janet is what used to be known as a Tall Gal. Not tall in the way supermodels are tall (they're what used to be known as Popsicle Sticks), but tall in the way that says she's the best living example yet of an Enjolé perfume commercial. She can bring home the bacon, fry it up in a pan—and make herself a tidy sandwich, too.

The bachelorette: Janet Reno was born in 1938. She married in . . . Never. She says she's shy and giggles to prove it. And you thought mystery women like this only existed in James Cain pulp novels? Meow!

The *Miami Vice* thing: In the mid-1980s, while Don Johnson and Philip Michael Thomas—all pink T-shirts and Italian loafers—were running around Miami pretending to be top cops, Reno was doing the real thing as Florida's state attorney general. Her glam-free style was the anecdote to the misperception that Crockett and Tubbs *were* Miami. It was Reno who *was* Miami. She represented the Great Silent Miami Majority—the locals who burn (not tan) and favor blousy floral button-downs to pink T-shirts. They are the putterers. And they *always* prevail over the trendoids. Today, Don Johnson's froufrou 1980s hair and pink T-shirts would get him laughed out of the city's hottest clubs. But Janet Reno's look? It's never in style—thus, *it never goes out of style*. Brilliant.

The spunk: In 1995, Reno disclosed she was afflicted with Parkinson's disease, a degenerative muscle condition. She said she intended to control the symptoms with medicine and continue with the work of her office. She did.

The good sense: When David E. Kelley was looking for a woman to play Janet Reno, his office first made a call to the Janet Reno. Was she up for the *Ally* cameo? Reno declined. Apparently even members of the va-va-voom Clinton Administration draw the line at showing themselves being picked up at a bar on national television.

people from *The Practice* are due in? This crowd needs some toughening up.

But, alas, no *Practice* people this time out. Just some precious nonsense about "smile therapy" and an uninvolving case involving a mad-bomber inmate (Thaddeus) and his devoted fiancée (Wilhoite).

The Fish-Whipper-Janet Reno triangle thing, at least, is fun—and audacious. Writing the U.S. Attorney General into a pick-up scene at a bar? Beautiful, if not impeachable.

Another random observation: This episode originally aired just weeks after President Clinton's Monica Lewinsky, um, situation came to a, um, head. And yet, there's Richard Fish cajoling Janet Reno with a jibe about sex-line calls from the White House. Quick turnaround or prescient thinking? Either way, impressive.

Background: Kelley eases up just a bit on the script front, sharing writing credit on an episode for the first time this season.

As noted previously, Linda Gehringer appeared on the 1992 pilot for *Picket Fences*. She also guested on a 1997 episode of *The Practice*.

Soundtrack notes: Carson lends Renee her vocal chords (again), dueting on a plaintive "For Your Love" with Kathleen Wilhoite. It sounds great (again), but serves to beg the question (again): Why the hell is Renee hanging around the Suffolk County Courthouse, when she should be on the road?

15. "Once in a Lifetime"

Original air date: 2/23/98
Story: David E. Kelley and Jeff Pinker; teleplay: David E. Kelley; director: Elodie Keene.

Guest cast: Richard Kiley (Seymore Little); Steven Flynn (Sam Little); Brigid Brannaugh (Paula); Phil Leeds (Judge Boyle); Bruce Nozick (Sam Little's attorney); Renee

Goldsberry, Vatrena King and Sy Smith (the Back-up Singers, formerly billed as the Ikettes)

The brief: The one about Ally and Billy working on a case together.

The verdict: ☆☆☆

Not one of the flashier episodes, but solid. The always good Richard Kiley is nothing less than that here as the famous artist who, in the twisted logic that makes *Ally*, well, *Ally*, wants to marry so he can devote himself to his first, dead wife. Not bad stuff.

Bad: MacNicol's Cage is uncaged—and unhinged. Dancing to Barry White, talking saliva secretions, toting a remote-control toilet flusher. Isn't there some form of Ritalin that would help this man? In lieu of that, is there a form of Ritalin that would help the audience? The prospect of Kelley pairing off Cage and Ally (they sort of date in this episode) and combining their abilities to annoy, is one that deserves a TV-MA rating. It's *that* frightening.

Another random observation: Consider yourself warned: Calista Flockhart's hair is now noticeably creeping down her neck.

Background: Richard Kiley's numerous credits include the original Broadway production of *The Man of La Mancha*, a great short-run NBC series called *A Year in the Life* (1987–88) and a 1994 guest stint on Kelley's *Picket Fences*.

Soundtrack notes: So, after five months, somebody (Flockhart's Ally) *finally* complains about the music at the

Vonda bar. Too disco or something, the line goes. Well, tough. It's a little late now. Vonda's been perfecting that 1970s singer-songwriter sound all season, and suddenly she's supposed to get contemporary? What, learn a new Meredith Wilson number or something? Talk about insensitive.

16. "Forbidden Fruits"
Original air date: 3/2/98
Writer: David E. Kelley; director: Jeremy Kagan.

Guest cast: Dina Meyer (Anna Flint); J. Patrick McCormack (U.S. Sen. James Foote); Marty Rackham (Joe Bepp); Gary Bullock (Judge Steele); Andrew Bloch (Mr. Colson); Elaine Giftos (Nancy Foote); Arnell Blanton (Attorney Williams); Jeff Sanders (Court Clerk); Helen Duffy (Foreperson); Dancing Baby (his very own creepy self).

The brief: The one about Georgia getting all cranky and telling Billy and Ally to just *do it*.

The verdict: ☆☆☆
Lots of positives in this episode. For starters, Billy tells Georgia to get a new haircut. (Somebody had to do it. . . .) For seconds, the Billy-Ally-Georgia thing finally bubbles over during a case involving a U.S. senator (McCormack), his new wife (Giftos) and the husband she dumped (Rackham) for the lawmaker. The show deftly avoids a *Moonlighting* (giving the viewers what they *think* they want; i.e., Dave and Maddie together) and (pretty much) stands firm with the position that Billy's going to be with Georgia—even if he still

kind of loves Ally. A Solomonlike decision by Kelley. A perfect way to close a door on a plot point that *is* getting a teensy bit tired—and at the same time, leave a window open for its possible return.

Background: So, what *is* the deal with Flockhart's skirt hemlines—the source of an on-air dig this episode by Dina Meyer's rival lawyer? Here was one take on the issue, as offered to E! Online's Ted Casablanca by an "unnamed" *Ally* cast member: "What [Flockhart] does is fold her skirt from the *inside*. She folds it over from the top—right before a scene. A little more each time." The powers-that-be at *Ally* later denounced that tidbit—so whatever. Let your own hemline be your guide.

More skirt stuff: The shortest ones are about fourteen inches "long," costume designer Rachael Stanley shared with *USA Today*.

Toothy Dina Meyer's other credits include the 1997 sci-fi bug flick, *Starship Troopers*.

Soundtrack notes: Vonda exists in voice only this episode, as for the first time all season there's not a single bar scene. (A walkout perhaps over the disco incident?)

Since an *Ally* without at least one major musical set-piece would be *The Practice*, the powers-that-be ensure that the Supremes' "Someday We'll Be Together" and Nat King Cole's "He'll Have to Go" get heavy, if unlikely, airplay in the courtroom scenes.

Lesson learned: Vonda camera-time or no, the apparent ban on any music recorded after 1979 remains in effect.

17. "Theme of Life"

Original air date: 3/9/98
Writer: David E. Kelley; director: Dennie Gordon.

Guest cast: Dyan Cannon (Whipper Cone); Tracey Ullman (Dr. Tracy Clark); Paul Guilfoyle (Harold Lane); Jesse L. Martin (Dr. Greg Butters); Liz Torres (Hanna Goldstein); Dawn Stern (Jeanette); John Fink (HMO executive): Linda Gehringer (Janet Reno); Don Perry (Foreman); Sally Wingert (Tour Guide); Bonnie Cheeseman, Marilyn Child, John Duerler, Geoffrey B. Nimmer and JoAnn Fregalette Jansen (Dancing Pedestrians); Dancing Baby (his own creepy self).

The brief: The one about theme songs—not TV ones, *person* ones.

The verdict: ☆☆☆

Another potential candidate for an *Ally* time capsule. Except if you were going to take the trouble to preserve this one, you'd have to do it right—and first edit out the Ally-and-Georgia boxing match subplot. Then you'd have an episode worthy of vacuum-sealing. Then you'd have Kelley at his wittiest (concocting Ally's abrasive, theme song–prescribing therapist). Then you'd have Kelley at his smartest (hiring Tracey Ullman to play said therapist). Then you'd have Kelley at his savviest (tapping—yet again—into one of those water cooler–friendly topics: So . . . what's *your* theme song?)

And best of all? Well, following your little cut-and-paste job, you wouldn't have Kelley at his weakest—giving in to his quirky creations and letting them run wild. Jealous Whipper

sniffing Fish's finger—a bloodhound on the trail of the Attorney General? Please. There are two things that *never* need be shown on television: (1) Dyan Cannon sniffing Greg Germann's finger, and (2) . . . Well, pretty much that first one again.

Other random observations: Good idea: Introduce a regular-guy love interest (Martin) to leaven the cumulative effect of the house loons.

Bad idea: Introduce a regular-guy love interest (Martin) and watch the house loons suddenly look *even loonier*.

Background: Theme-song therapy apparently is a creation of the one, the only David E. Kelley. "He thinks of [things] before they happen. He's prescient," Jeffrey Kramer told Associated Press.

Kelley's vision took. After the "Theme of Life" broadcast, Oprah Winfrey turned over an episode of her daytime talk show to the topic of personal theme songs. One of her audience's favorites, according to Associated Press? Gloria Gaynor's "I Will Survive."

Jane Krakowski's theme-song pick for her Elaine character? "'I Cain't Say No,'" she told *Teen People*. "It's about how she can't resist any fella that comes along," she said.

Familiar face Liz Torres has done *everything*—from *Mary Tyler Moore* spin-off *Phyllis* (1975–76) to Discover Card commercials.

Eerie: Veteran actor and *Sea Hunt* star Lloyd Bridges (referenced briefly in this episode by Ullman's Dr. Clark) died March 10, 1998—the day after "Theme of Life" first aired.

Soundtrack notes: Kelley's obsession with baby boomer–era music finally yields a true find: The Cufflinks' "Tracy." Bouncy, peppy, not overused—yup, this *is* a song people play in their heads. And the man's dead right about something else here, too: People *should* dance in the street (provided they abide by the appropriate pedestrian signals). Maybe they shouldn't necessarily do it to "Tell Him" (*way* overused), but they should do it.

"Tell Him," by the way, was Kelley's first choice for the series' theme song, Vonda Shepard told the *Washington Post*.

Also, keen lyrics-observers will note that the ditty that Flockhart's Ally first proposes as her personal theme song— the one shot down as being, well, lousy—is none other than "Searchin' My Soul."

18. "The Playing Field"
Original air date: 3/16/98
Writer: David E. Kelley; director: Jonathan Pontell.

Guest cast: Tracey Ullman (Dr. Tracy Clark); Jesse L. Martin (Dr. Greg Butters); Josh Evans (Oren Koolie); Christine Dunford (Eva Curry); Wrenn T. Brown (Mr. Stone); Michael Winters (Judge Spitt); Shea Farrell (Mr. Tyler); Miriam Flynn (Karen Koolie); Jerry Sroka (Joel); Renee Goldsberry, Vatrena King and Sy Smith (Back-up Singers).

The brief: The one about the little-kid lawyer (Evans).

The verdict: ☆☆
A good but strange episode.

Good: Courtney Thorne-Smith ditches the *Melrose Place* do. Strange: She replaces it with something presumably spotted on a model in a Stove Top Stuffing ad. Either that, or the blades were really dull. (Translation: It's a tad, um, dowdy.)

More good: Josh Evans is wonderful as the pouty nine-year-old attorney trying to squeeze accident-claim money out of Martin's Dr. Butters. More strange: This show is already so strange there is absolutely *nothing* strange about a pouty nine-year-old attorney. It's going to take more than that to impress us at this point.

Background: Kelley mined child-prodigy ground before, in *Doogie Howser, M.D.* (1989–93). Lest that be forgotten, he works in a *Doogie* reference.

No slight intended to the diminutive Evans, but this episode came in a little, um, short. When the show cut together, it wasn't quite its usual 45-minute self. No biggie. Fox happily responded by padding out the hour with extra commercials, according to the *New York Times*.

Transcript of actual phone call placed to the chamber of commerce in Poughkeepsie, New York—"Poughkeepsie" being the latest word upgraded to *Ally* catchphrase status with this episode:

> CALLER: Um, I was wondering, does this place have anything to do with *Ally McBeal?*
> CHAMBER: No.
> CALLER: (*hopeful*) No *Ally* tours or anything?
> CHAMBER: No.

CALLER: You guys don't have *anything* to do with the
show . . . ?
CHAMBER: Poughkeepsie is a place. . . .
CALLER: (*disappointed*) Oh. . . .

According to the official Poughkeepsie Web site, the town's name is Native American for "the Reed-Covered Lodge by the Little Water Place." Thus ends our geography/language lesson.

Soundtrack notes: Following the theme-song blowout, nothing too remarkable this time out, save for a good (if obvious) gag with *The Wizard of Oz*'s "Munchkinland."

19. "Happy Birthday, Baby"
Original air date: 4/6/98
Writer: David E. Kelley; director: Thomas Schlamme.

Guest cast: Jesse L. Martin (Dr. Greg Butters); Harriet Sansom Harris (Cheryl Bonner); Barry Miller (Mark Henderson); Alaina Reed Hall (Judge Witt); Danny Borowicz (Officer); Roberta West (Foreperson).

The brief: The one about Ally's twenty-eighth birthday.

The verdict: ☆☆☆
If there's one single cosmic reason why *Ally* is bound to fail in the comedy category at the Primetime Emmys, it's this episode. Sometimes there's just *nothing* funny about the show or its characters. And when an episode like "Happy Birthday, Baby" comes along, it makes you wonder if there *ever was*

anything funny. Should you laugh at a character like Ally—by turns a delusional and deeply unhappy young woman? Should you laugh when it becomes clear that the series is intent on making her worse—not better?

Well, go ahead. Laugh. It *is* just TV, after all. But let's also admit that there used to be a hopefulness about both *Ally* and Ally. And, here, it's clear that there is no hope—there's just varying degrees of desperation. Sometimes the desperation leads the characters to silly, funny things. And sometimes the desperation leads the characters to desperate, sad things. Flockhart's flailing, forced peppy pajama dance here is one of the latter. What's on the screen is still good TV, to be sure. It's just not *funny* TV.

Other random observations: The *Night Court* trap: About every fourth episode of *Night Court* (1984–92), John Larroquette's boorish prosecutor character would learn a valuable lesson in what it means to be a good person. Then the very next episode, he'd be back to being boorish. His character had no collective memory. Jane Krakowski's Elaine is a lot like that. For seemingly the umpteenth time this season (including this episode), we learn that beneath her obnoxious exterior Elaine just wants to be loved—then she goes right back to being obnoxious. Grr.

The Vera syndrome: There go Krakowski and Carson again—selling songs like the seasoned pros their characters *aren't*. This time they're joined onstage by guest star Jesse L. Martin—another Broadway ringer who makes his character's choice in careers (medicine over music) seem more than a tad dubious.

Background: Well, at least someone admits the series' talent showcases are a tad odd: "I never expected to be singing on TV, much less on a law show," Krakowski told *USA Today*.

The series rolls out a new opening-credits sequence with this episode. It features footage of all the main cast members—and suggests the slow, but subtle shift from Ally! Ally! Ally! to ensemble.

When his hair was wilder and he was younger, Barry Miller (here, foot-fetishist client Mark Henderson) played one of the angst-ridden *Fame* kids in the 1980 movie. He went on to costar in the 1990–91 ABC lawyer series, *Equal Justice*.

Soundtrack notes: Krakowski, Carson and Vonda cook in a rendition of that old perfume commercial jingle, better known as Leiber and Stoller's "I'm a Woman." And while it's tough to quibble that something's too good—it's *too* good. Ditto for Carson and Martin's luscious duet on "Don't." Nothing but plot constraints are holding these people back from cutting demos and hightailing it to New York or Los Angeles.

20. "The Inmates" [Part One]
Original air date: 4/27/98
Writer: David E. Kelley; director: Michael Schultz.

Guest cast: Dylan McDermott (Bobby Donnell); Lisa Gay Hamilton (Rebecca Washington); Steve Harris (Eugene Young); Camryn Manheim (Ellenor Frutt); Kelli Williams (Lindsay Dole); Donna Murphy (Marie Hanson); Kelly

Connell (Dr. Peters); Isaiah Washington (Michael Rivers); Alaina Reed Hall (Judge Witt); Michael Brandon (D.A. Adam Dawson); David Burke (Harry); Tony Amendola (Judge Swan); Al Pugliese (Joel Hurt); Daniel Dae Kim (Officer Pratt); George Cedar (Judge Harker); Paul Jenkins (Detective Kale); Renee Goldsberry, Vatrena King and Sy Smith (Back-up Singers); Eric Cohen (Dancing Twin #1); Steve Cohen (Dancing Twin #2).

"Axe Murderer" [Part Two—As aired on *The Practice*]
Original air date: 4/27/98
Writer: David E. Kelley and Todd Ellis Kessler; director: Dennis Smith.

The Practice **guest cast:** Calista Flockhart (Ally McBeal); Gil Bellows (Billy Thomas); Donna Murphy (Marie Hanson); J. C. MacKenzie (Dr. Fred Spivak); Kelly Connell (Dr. Peters); Michael Brandon (D.A. Adam Dawson); Reni Santoni (Roland Mapp); Daniel Dae Kim (Officer Pratt); Lynn Hamilton (Judge Fulton); Shunil Bailey (Guslet); John Kendall (Glenn); Janet S. Blake (Slauson); Dan Schaffer (Dr. Seymore Holt); Maira Price (Dr. Elaine Madison); Randy Kovitz (Dr. Marcus Johnson); Mijanou van der Woude (Reporter #1).

The brief: The *Ally* meets *Practice* episodes.

The verdict: ☆☆☆ (total for both episodes)
On paper, this looks like a mismatch. *The Practice* people—all serious and *real*—are going to make the *Ally* "kids," as they're

referred to here, look like the bratty caricatures they've become. But in reality, it doesn't work that way. In reality, the lightweights hold their own—in their own way.

And in reality, you learn exactly why *Ally* gets the ratings and *The Practice* doesn't; and why *The Practice* gets the Emmy and *Ally* doesn't.

It's all about sex.

The *Ally* people are too young and pretty and female to be taken seriously—by anyone except viewers. The viewers don't have axes to grind or colleagues to impress. They just want to laugh when Flockhart gets pummeled by the elevator doors.

The *Practice* people, meanwhile, are predominately older and realer-looking (except for leading man McDermott) and male. Critics and industry types weaned on Stephen Bochco dramas love to take a show like this seriously. They understand it—it's a lawyer show, a tough, Bochconian lawyer show. Even has a picture of a gun in the opening credits— heck, it's gotta mean business, it's gotta be important. The only people not drawn devoutly to this material are the viewers. To them, it's good. It's fine. It's kind of like other lawyer shows they've seen before—maybe better. But bottom line: It's not *special*.

If this crossover story line proves nothing else, it proves that *Ally* is special.

Kelley piles on the nuts in the *Ally* half of the story. Every quirk, every catchphrase, every jokey special-effect is here—times three. It's supposed to make the *Ally* people look ridiculous, and it does. But it also makes the Cage/Fish side of the equation look more appealing—more inventive. Sorry,

but sober, streetwise Bobby Donnell types are as old as the dawn of *Hill Street Blues*. Being "streetwise" on TV is not a novelty. Being "streetwise" is not a virtue. But being John Cage? Or being Ally McBeal? That's some kind of perverse bravery. It almost—*almost*—makes you appreciate the nose whistle.

Briefly, the case that draws the two camps together involves a rich woman (Murphy) who apparently axed her husband while under the influence of Lizzie Borden.

The *Ally* half took heat from critics who locked on to Flockhart's wide-eyed, shoulder-chewing turn as the criminal-skittish Ms. McBeal. A damning portrait of the professional woman, they charged. Bogus. A damning portrait of one woman—Ally McBeal. And back in Episode No. 5 Ally McBeal won the right to be stupid. So get off her back.

The *Practice* half got the better reviews—and rightly so; it had the meaty ax-murderer trial. Per usual, its hour (with Flockhart and Bellows along for the ride) was solid TV. It was coherent. It was delightfully free of old Fifth Dimension covers.

But it was also so astoundingly *normal*.

It was not *Ally*.

Second opinions: " . . . The mere presence of Donnell—brusque, lawyerly and all business—sombers and tones down the show, to the extent that it's far from *Ally McBeal* at its best. And this gets much worse when the plot continues on *The Practice.* . ."—*Los Angeles Times*

"The marriage [of the two series] is strong, but it is not perfect."—*Hollywood Reporter*

Background: Kelley told *USA Today* he initially thought a crossover would be "tonally incompatible." He got over it.

In the end, Kelley couldn't resist the chance to let some of *Ally*'s buzz bounce off the low-rated *Practice*. "As a parent of two [TV] children I'm frustrated for *The Practice*. They're doing good work, too, and they wonder if anybody is paying attention," he told the *New York Post*.

Fox affiliates griped early and often about Kelley's crossover dream. They didn't want Fox viewers tuning out local 10:00 P.M. newscasts to switch over to ABC and *The Practice*. Accordingly, Fox did not promote the two-part nature of the broadcast.

Meanwhile at hit-starved ABC, the network ecstatically teased: "[The] trendiest lawyer in America is coming to *The Practice*."

This was not the first *Ally* crossover of the season. Earlier, a scene from the series popped up on a TV screen in the Kelley-created *Chicago Hope* on CBS. In Season No. 2, a scene from *The Practice* plays in the backround in *Ally McBeal*.

A highlight of the *Ally*–*Practice* summit was the anticipated "skinny-off" between Flockhart and Lara Flynn Boyle. Boyle, herself the target of weighty snipes in the past, vouched for Flockhart's own good health in *TVGen*: "It's like people are just looking for something. They're saying, 'Well, she may be a good actress and her show is successful, but look at how thin she is. There must be a problem there.'"

Donna Murphy is a two-time Tony winner—for Stephen Sondheim's *Passion* (1994) and the 1996 revival of *The King and I*.

Kelly Connell is a veteran character actor and a regular member of the Kelley company. He played Carter Pike on *Picket Fences* and guest-starred on an episode of *Chicago Hope*.

Soundtrack notes: Vonda is, of course, not allowed to practice on *The Practice*. Those guys eat singer-songwriters for lunch. But on the *Ally* side, it's Dancing Twins business as usual. Let the nondescript sounds of the seventies play on.

21. "Being There"
Original air date: 5/4/98
Writer: David E. Kelley; director: Mel Damski.

Guest cast: Isaiah Washington (Michael Rivers); Michael Easton (Glenn); Gibby Brand (Judge McGough); Eric McCormack (D.A. Kevin Kepler); Erica Nicole Dickerson (Young Renee); Shannon Welles and Herb Borben (Elderly Couple); Patricia Tate (Bailiff); Earl K. Kim (Foreperson).

The brief: The one about (*a*) Georgia maybe being pregnant, and (*b*) boyfriend-bashing Renee maybe getting convicted. (And, nope, neither one happens. No room for [real] babies or prisoners on this show—they might be good influences on the other characters.)

The verdict: ☆☆
Well, with no *Practice* people around to make these clowns look good anymore, we return to our normal mode of criticism. . . .

How appropriate to kick off this episode with the extra-special "world premiere broadcast" of Vonda's "Searchin' My

Soul" video. After all, the people, er, caricatures, on display here have all the depth of music-video models.

Now Cage's shoes squeak (?!?) Now Elaine wiretaps offices (?!?) Granted, this thing is supposed to be a comedy, but it's not supposed to be freakin' *Gilligan's Island*. This is a show that also aspires to drama. And the problem is, those twin missions don't mesh here. Billy and Georgia—even the slightly off-balance Renee—seem off in their own world—a world called Planet Sanity. It's a nice place to visit. In fact, it'd be a nice place to stay. But, alas, it's not to be. Here's Elaine with her freezer-equipped jockey shorts. Yeesh.

Another random observation: Brownie points: The overall yuckiness of the episode threatens to (but doesn't) subvert real nice work by Bellows and Thorne-Smith. Thorne-Smith, in particular, turns in her most assured work of the season, even operating under the handicap that is *that haircut.*

Background: "Searchin' My Soul" climbed as high as No. 14 on *Billboard*'s Top 40 singles charts.

Eric McCormack found *Entertainment Weekly* magazine fame by playing yet another TV lawyer, Will Truman, on the NBC sitcom, *Will & Grace* (1998–).

Soundtrack notes: Even at its most cloying, there is an important public service *Ally* performs—it keeps alive the goofy, unbridled spirit of the musical. Here, it's a law-firm dance number to "Wedding Bell Blues."

22. "Alone Again"

Original air date: 5/11/98
Writer: David E. Kelley; director: Dennis Dugan.

Guest cast: Dyan Cannon (Whipper Cone); Cynthia Stevenson (Hayley Chisolm); McNally Sagal (Mary Halliday); Michael Hagerty (Michael Huttle); Gibby Brand (Judge McGough); Neal Learner (George Pullman); Jocko Marcellino (Prison Guard); Dabbs Greer (Vincent Robbins); Renee Goldsberry, Vatrena King and Sy Smith (Back-up Singers); Landry Barb (Clerk); Bill Bishop (Foreman); Bill Finkelstein (William).

The brief: The one about . . . Um, the one about . . . *Something*, for sure. Just not anything memorable.

The verdict: ☆☆

To paraphrase Ally in the cold opener, How stupid is this? A case about a guy (Greer) who breaks out of prison on a trampoline? Whatever. The senses are numb to this nonsense now. Ultimately, you either accept the *Ally* universe or you don't. There's no use fighting it. If Kelley's going to write a bit where Cage controls his stuttering by invoking the name of New York City's mayor, then so be it. That's just the way things are going to be here. If you're distressed, move on. There's always *Monday Night Football*.

Background: The always appealing Cynthia Stevenson (here as the appealing unrequited law-school love of Cage) is one of TV's most familiar faces—and one of its least lucky perform-

ers. Her projects are rarely up to her talent (not the case here). Credits include the 1995–96 NBC sitcom, *Hope and Gloria*.

Dabbs Greer was the kindly Reverend Alden on *Little House on the Prairie* (1974–83).

Soundtrack notes: Walking-and-Thinking Watch: Cage, to a Vonda rendition of Gilbert O'Sullivan's 1972 hit, "Alone Again (Naturally)." Befitting the serious nature of this vaunted *Ally* assignment, the shoe-squeaking shtick is put on hold. Cage just *walks*. Do not begrudge blessings, however small.

23. "These Are the Days"
Original air date: 5/18/98
Writer: David E. Kelley; director: Jonathan Pontell.

Guest cast: Dylan McDermott (Bobby Donnell); Willie Garson (Alan Farmer); Richard Schiff (Bernie Gilson); Phil Leeds (Judge Boyle); Albert Hall (Judge Walsh); Lee Wilkof (D.A. Nixon); Rhonda Dotson (Julie Martin); Ken Abraham (Hendrix); Bob Gunton (Michaelson); Gerry Vichi (Foreman).

The brief: The one about Billy and Georgia having sex in the conference room.

The verdict: ☆☆
Strange. An episode that, up until the last few minutes, plays like a perfunctory, middle-of-the-season outing, rather than the closer of a remarkable first season. Not even the stunt casting of Dylan McDermott—his *Practice* guy is there to work a case involving a heart-swap transplant—helps. (Zippo

in the chemistry department, too, between Flockhart and McDermott.)

But because Kelley rarely goes hitless, there's a revved-up Billy and Georgia to keep things interesting. The conference-room sex scene is hardly the focus of the episode—but it's the keeper. A nice way of letting two characters cut loose without forcing them to cut all ties to the rational world.

Another random observation: Paging Martha Stewart: The person who does Thorne-Smith's hair must have a cousin who decorates her TV home. You'd think it would be a treat to get a rare, extended look at the Thomases' place. You'd *think* that. Then you see it and you realize it's best not to stare at salmon-pink (?!) walls, lest you impair your own sense of good taste.

Background: The shot of Courtney Thorne-Smith's bare, left corner butt cheek—brief and chaste though it may be—is a surprising first nude scene for oft-raunchy Fox. (As is the rule for networks, sniggering sex-talk is preferred by executives to actual displays of body parts.)

According to *USA Today*, the Thorne-Smith bare bum scene revealed a touch more skin when originally shot.

Ally goes out on top (or near it): a 9.7 rating, placing twenty-first in the final week of the 1997–98 season.

Soundtrack notes: "Neighborhood" frames a would-be weepy look back on the past eight months of the *Ally* people's TV lives. You could accuse the show of wallowing in premature nostalgia, but then you could accuse this book of the same thing. So we thought it best not to mention the whole thing. Okay?

Chapter 14

The Second Season (1998–99)

REGULAR CAST
Calista Flockhart (Ally McBeal)
Courtney Thorne-Smith (Georgia Thomas)
Greg Germann (Richard Fish)
Lisa Nicole Carson (Renee Radick)
Jane Krakowski (Elaine Vassal)
Vonda Shepard (herself)
with Peter MacNicol (John Cage)
and Gil Bellows (Billy Thomas)
Portia de Rossi (Nelle Porter)*
Lucy Liu (Ling Woo)*
Not listed in main credits

Season overview: And so it comes to pass that in the show's sophomore year, everybody gets fat and happy—Calista Flockhart and her TV alter ego excepted. And, yes, the pun *is* intended.

Long-running, successful television series present interesting insights into the lives of the nouveau riche. Take a look at any show's first season and, assuming the cast is mainly comprised of no-name types, you'll find a gaggle of young,

eager, underfed actors with aim-to-please haircuts. Think *thirtysomething*, circa 1987. Fast-forward to *thirtysomething*, circa 1990, and you'll find a gaggle of older, thicker actors with shaggy, who-cares haircuts, and waistlines that suggest the ability to spring for steak and lobster—for breakfast. (*Star Trek* is also a good study in this phenomenon. And not just for William Shatner's expanding/contracting gut. The Enterprise captain apparently wasn't the only one partaking in the good life.)

Often the spoils of newfound wealth extend to the production itself—the clothes get better, the sets get better, the budgets get bigger. *Ally McBeal* is no exception to the rule—in fact, it's an advanced *example* of the rule. After only one season, the powers-that-be moved the production from Hollywood's old-school Ren-Mar Studios (onetime home to *I Love Lucy*) to Hollywood's ultimate destination of the recently anointed class, the beach—specifically, Manhattan Beach. There, cast and crew enjoy spacious new digs—and the Ally and Renee characters enjoy a spacious new beach-front penthouse. The penthouse set is never explained or discussed on the show. These things are just understood.

So are these things: In *Ally*'s Season No. 2, Greg Germann's trademark Fish vests get fancier; Courtney Thorne-Smith's hair gets (slightly) more stylish; Peter MacNicol's ambitions get bigger (he directs Episode No. 3, "Fools Night Out," original air date: 9/28/98). They are the perks—the byproducts—of hit-show status. Overall, the show gets bigger and broader (Cage's pet frog silliness); riskier (Ally and Georgia's play-acting lip lock in Episode No. 6, "You Never Can Tell," original air date: 11/23/98); prettier

Watching *Ally*

People watch *Diagnosis: Murder*. (Really.) People *experience* a show like *Ally McBeal*. The difference? One is allegedly pleasant TV (as well as superb background noise). The other is apparently a social rite of passage.

To wit, from the East Coast to the West Coast, *Ally* viewing rituals have been observed on a near weekly basis. In Washington, D.C., a restaurant called Legal Sea Foods marked the 1997–98 season by dispensing free drink refills every time Greg Germann's scaly lawyer character uttered the blurb-friendly catchphrase "Bygones." On other nights, the eatery sponsored an Ally look-alike pageant and trivia contests.

In Los Angeles, the *New Times'* Glenn Gaslin detailed the *"Ally McBeal Drinking Game,"* wherein participants guzzle when, yes, "Bygones" is uttered—or when any other number of *Ally* standbys occur.

The games are further testament to *Ally's* pop-culture appeal. Even though, when you think of it, if there's a show that demands being viewed under the influence of a cheap-booze buzz, it's *Diagnosis: Murder*.

(the introduction of eye-candy attorney Nelle Porter in Episode No. 1, "The Real World," original air date: 9/14/98). Indeed, the only part of the show that seems to contract is Flockhart and Ally.

Early in the season, as anorexia rumors swirl, Flockhart's physical appearance is ghoulish incentive to tune in. ("Oh, look! She's gonna turn sideways!") If the show itself is concerned by the actress's weight, it doesn't let on. The wardrobe department outfits her in tight jeans, tight T-shirts and the standard microskirt—viewers' opinions be damned.

Once you get past (if you get past) the Calista Flockhart guessing game (Is she or isn't she?), you notice the *real* secret of the second season: *Ally McBeal* isn't really *Ally McBeal* anymore. It's *Ally McBeal's Friends*. Or maybe even *The Friends of Ally McBeal*.

With its already-large cast beefed up by the addition of two new members (Portia de Rossi and Lucy Liu), the show takes on a greater-than-ever ensemble slant. The firm no longer revolves around Ally's life. The firm and its various wack-jobs function independently of Ms. McBeal. David E. Kelley shamelessly dotes on Cage. He plays up Porter. He gamely tries to make Georgia and Billy seem mildly interesting. (Sad but true, and increasingly apparent: Bellows's stick-in-the-mud attorney wouldn't be compelling if he were lit on fire.) When Flockhart's character gets stuck in a toilet (in the episode "Just Looking," original air date: 11/16/98), it plays not so much as comedy, but as a desperate cry for attention— "Please! Somebody! Remember me?!? *The one who was on the #@*#&! cover of* Time *magazine!*"

Progress claims another victim.

Highlights: John Ritter guest-stars as canned magazine editor George Madison. (His first episode: "It's My Party," original air date: 10/19/98—aka The Flat-Out Stupid One Where Ally Is Arrested for Wearing a Too-Short Skirt in Court.) Kelley gives in to his baser *Three's Company* instincts and concocts a scene in which Flockhart leaps—crotch first— into Ritter's face. Fox gives in to its usual *Married . . . With Children* instincts and promotes the scene heavily during the

World Series. The result? Record ratings—and another great moment in TV history.

Phil Leeds makes his final appearance in the episode "Happy Trails" (original air date: 11/9/98). The installment—about the death of his character, Judge "Happy" Boyle—was built around a Leeds scene cut from the season opener, "The Real World." After Leeds's death, Kelley decided to resurrect the footage for an episode paying homage to Leeds/Boyle. (A stand-in was used for the sequence in which Boyle keels over on the bench as, unfortunately, Leeds was already too dead to do the bit himself.)

The verdict: If John Cage floats your boat, you probably dig the new Ally-light *Ally*. If characters approximating life on Planet Earth are more your thing, *Monday Night Football* is looking like an attractive option. You may not be able to wholly relate to a three-hundred-pound linebacker, but at least you can take comfort in the fact that the guy won't moan on (and on and on and on . . .) about a *frog*.

Final Summation

The question is, Is *Ally* good TV? Of course it is. David E. Kelley can write. The actors can act. The crew can turn out a polished mini-movie, twenty-plus times a year. Even in its off weeks it's worth a dozen *Nash Bridges*es.

Did it live up to its early promise? Only Kelley can answer that. If *you* thought the show was going to be about Everywoman but devolved into Some Nutty Kook, then it didn't live up to *your* expectations. You can only surmise that

Kelley—calling every shot—is doing what he wants. So maybe it *was* his plan to see how far he could take out-there characters.

Were the shows better the "old" way? Yes. Pre–Dancing Baby, Ally was a person. Post–Dancing Baby, she was a goner—off in her own private world of impossibly cute pajamas, impossible-to-wear shoes and increasingly banal observations.

So big deal. People—well, characters—change. The good ones, anyway. Al Bundy, for instance, never, ever changed—not one bit. And where did it get him, except a decade-plus in *Married . . . With Children* hell?

The important thing is to evolve, and yet not lose sight of the original mission.

And hey, John Ritter—Jack Tripper, his very own self—got around to doing a guest stint. So, really—how far off base did things really get?

Appendix A
Web sites

As if TV weren't a big enough sap on our free time, scientist types invented the Web. Through this triumph of technological know-how, millions of modem-equipped global citizens are now able to take their tubeland thoughts one step further. When mere break-time chatter ("Hey, did you catch last night's show?) won't suffice, the Internet allows the cyberfan to ask, "Hey, did you catch last night's show?" in convenient print form. Isn't it a great time to be alive? Or, more to the point of *Ally McBeal*, isn't it a great time to be a TV show?

Below is a highly subjective list of some of the top sites that *Ally* aficionados have contributed to the online universe. Owing to its highly subjective nature, it features twenty-seven sites. Why twenty-seven? Because anything ending in a 5 or 0 seemed, well, too official. Therefore, we present:

The *Ally* 27

THE OFFICIALS

1. Ally McBeal [Fox]
http://www.foxworld.com/ally/

Bright, colorful and chock-full of bouncy thought-bubbles. In other words, this Fox-built site is every bit as zippy and cloying as its pet show. A good source for comprehensive cast biographies (provided you don't want to know precisely how old everybody is—networks are loath to rat

out their stars' birthdays) and ultra-detailed plot synopses. All this, plus tons of photos, some of which move and, sort of, um, hop—well, it's hard to describe, let's just say the effect is, you know, cute. Like the show.

Gets points for being a Dancing Baby–Free Zone. Loses points for being slow to update its info. Almost a month into Season No. 2, for instance, there was virtually no sign of it here.

2. Official Vonda Shepard Web Site

http://www.vesperalley.com/

Brought to you by the folks who have released (and/or rereleased) Ms. Shepard's solo albums. And while Vesper Alley may not be the label behind Shepard's *Songs from "Ally McBeal"* soundtrack (that's Sony), make no mistake, the company is all too happy for the hit-show association. And why not? A quick check of this site—with its jam-packed tour-date schedules and radio-station playlist updates—is a testament to what *Ally* means to Vonda.

Best site feature: Extensive links to (seemingly) everything ever published about Shepard during her break-out year of 1998. Read 'em 'til your eyeballs bug out. And if you do, then the site will have you right where it wants you—tired, weary and open to the prospect of ordering soothing Vonda CDs online.

3. The Official Dancing Twins Web site

http://members.aol.com/allytwins/

Here it is. In all its—or rather, their—glory. As noted in the cast biography section, this is the authorized cyberhome of actors/jugglers Steve and Eric Cohen, aka the Dancing Twins. The site is about what you'd expect: pictures of them getting funky; a brief history of how they got funky; and links to articles talking about them being funky. This site also promises to be the place for all your Dancing Twins merchandising needs—T-shirts, etc. The stuff wasn't available at last click, but one can dream. Best feature of all: *No dancing babies!*

THE ESSENTIALS

4. The Ally McBeal *FAQ*

http://ccwf.cc.utexas.edu/~sikkid/allyfaq.html

The place to start for the *Ally* newbie. This utilitarian "Frequently Asked Questions" page covers the basics of the show—cast, locations, trivia. It even attempts to soberly address whether the fictional lawyers of Cage/Fish and Associates in any way resemble real lawyers. (The site-keeper's educated guess: TV is taking liberties. Lots of them.) The best reason to log on here? The links. This is a great one-stop, catch-all for *Ally*-specific links, for *Ally*-actor links, for *Ally*-everything links.

5. Dana's Ally McBeal *Page*

http://allymcbeal.tktv.net

Incredibly comprehensive. Also, this thing is updated like a mother. No "we didn't get around to the new season" apologies here. There are even lines on upcoming, unseen episodes. For your reading pleasure, there's a bunch of links to magazine articles, online chats and published *Ally* what-not. How complete is this site? It even has its own search engine. It works, too. When all else fails (and it's likely anything here will), subscribe to its weekly newsletter.

6. Arthur Tham's Ally McBeal *Site*

http://amcb.hypermart.net

My, but how this show does inspire devotion. Here's another site to behold—wholly complete and diligently updated. (It's also got that nifty site-search engine action going for it. Plus, its own *Ally* newsletter, too—available via e-mail subscription.) Then there are the extra-special specials: The fan fiction (wherein fans contribute their own *Ally* tales); the *Ally McBeal* Stress Reduction Kit (wherein users are invited to bang their skulls against their computer screens, à la their favorite head-banging TV heroine); and the tops—the parody/faux Web site for Ally's fictional law firm, Cage/Fish and Associates. All in all, a big must-see.

7. *Almost Human's* Ally McBeal *Page*

http://www.geocities.com/TelevisionCity/Set/8532/allymcbeal.html

This site knows what designer clothes Calista Flockhart dons as Ally—plus where to buy them. Enough said? Trust this, if Flockhart's TV lawyer had a TV-land Social Security card, its number would be noted here—everything else is: late-breaking news, article links, where-to-buy info on CDs and videos featuring cast members, and, best of all, viewer polls. What are your top five *Ally* episodes of all time? (All right, granted we're not dealing with an expansive legacy. But still. . . .) Fans from Bowling Green, Ohio, to County Down, Northern Ireland, weigh in with their verdicts. A lively interactive community.

8. Ally McBeal: *An Episode Guide*

http://www.xnet.com/~djk/AllyMcBeal_1.shtml

This above address is for the small *Ally* outpost on the must-bookmark Episode Guides Page site: http://www.xnet.com/~fergus/titles.shtml. The Episode Guides Page keeps log sheets on more than 1,000 TV series. There, you'll find original air dates, writing and directing credits, as well as guest-cast listings. Straightforward and accurate with no fussy extras. The Jack Webb of Web pages: "Just the facts, ma'am." (If you're looking for plot summaries, go to the Fox site. There's no opinion there, but there's enough detail to make you feel like you watched the episode again—or for the first time.)

THE LINKMEISTERS

9. *The* Ally McBeal *Webring*

http://www.webring.org/cgi-bin/webring?ring=allyring;list

A Webring is a collection of links—nothing more, nothing less. Actually, there's very little "less" about this site. At last look, there were sixty-five—count 'em, sixty-five—*Ally*-related Web sites listed here (including ones for individual performers and, yes, that freakin' Dancing Baby). At last

inspection, not all of the noted sites were up and still running (nor were all of them in English), but still. . . .

Ye gods. Sixty-five?!?! Prepare to be astounded.

10. "Ally McBeal's" Little Black Book

http://www.amherst.edu/~lebaer/amcbeal/menu.html

Remember how just a second ago it sounded like sixty-five *Ally* links was a lot? Ha! By the summer of 1998, this site had 198—or, as an overenthusiastic sportscaster with a firm grasp of the obvious might intone, "*That's almost two hundred!*" Yes, indeed it is. Now, how do you accumulate almost two hundred *Ally* links? You get connected—to bulletin boards, to show sites, to episode-guides sites, to *Ally* articles, to actor-specific sites (including a Courtney Thorne-Smith one that's so "updated" it notes the star has—news flash!—decided to depart *Melrose Place*). If the thought of wading through 198 links gives you a brain cramp, skip right to "The Real McBeal"—it's the site's own collection of "best of" sites. At a recent check, that amounted to very manageable twentysomething.

11. The Crazy About Calista Webring

http://www.geocities.com/TelevisionCity/Studio/2307/webring.html

A quite decent one-stop surf shop for Flockhart faithful, with links to (last count) seven actress-friendly sites.

THE QUIRKMEISTERS

12. Lawgirl Rants: Ally McBeal

http://www.lawgirl.com/ally.shtml/

Lawgirl is the not-so secret identity of Los Angeles–based attorney Jodi L. Sax, or so the Lawgirl site tells us. By day, Lawgirl specializes in copyright- and entertainment-related legal matters. By night (presumably), she watches *Ally McBeal*—and rolls her eyes. (A little, anyway. In truth, she *does* like the show.) But if you want a from-the-trenches take on how Ms.

McBeal stacks up in the real world (and the real courtroom), check out Lawgirl's reality-checking essay: "What's the Deal with Ally McBeal?" A very fun read. And, no, Lawgirl does not think Jane Krakowski's annoying secretary character would last more than a day on the job. We're shocked—shocked!

13. The Sports Fan's Guide to Ally McBeal

http://www.geocities.com/Hollywood/Hills/3384/AllyMain.htm

How do you distinguish your *Ally* site from the masses? Get a gimmick. The one offered here does nicely. Banking that the online community is a safe haven for sharing deep, dark secrets, this site is dedicated to *Monday Night Football* and/or pro-wrestling fans (read: guys) who yearn to channel surf over to *Ally*. The best read here: The "True Confessions" section, where manly men post their *Ally*-related trials and tribulations. Make no mistake, though, this is a guy's-guy site—it ain't all touchy-feely. In fact, it's very much a den for "babe" watchers. The site's top-ranked babe? Ms. Flockhart, but of course.

14. Barb's Ally McBeal Page

http://www.flash.net/~jerryg/barbsallypage.html

So, your friend missed last week's episode and you don't know anyone else who watched and you've just to got to share your gripes with someone? Then Barb is your virtual friend. You can't talk back to her (although, there's always e-mail), but you can drop in on her monologues—all about, of course, the state of *Ally*. No mere episode guide, this is an opinion guide. All episodes (or at least those dating back to March 1998) are critiqued in a series of columns that are typically pithy, freewheeling and off-the-cuff. How to be sure if she's a legitimate voice? Check out these opinions: (1) She was deeply disturbed by the length of Courtney Thorne-Smith's pre-haircut hair; (2) she was nonplussed by Thorne-Smith's post-haircut hair; and (3) she was nonplussed by Season No. 2's early episodes. The verdict: On the money.

15. Ally McBeal *My Life*

http://sqx.simplenet.com/tv/ally/people/index.html

Sort of informational, sort of spooky. Read Ally McBeal's reputedly inner thoughts as projected by the sitekeeper. The entries are handled with a fair amount of wit, but they do make you wonder: Is it possible to become too "one" with a TV character? When you start anticipating the hopes and aspirations of a make-believe person, is it maybe time to move on to something else? Like, a different show? Oh well, that concern is for others. In this site, die-hard fans have a fun resource.

Note: Don't go looking for obligatory cast bios here. In this corner of cyberspace, no one plays Billy. Billy is Billy. (Cue: *Twilight Zone* theme.)

16. The Ally McBeal *Quote Page*

http://www.geocities.com/Hollywood/Studio/3233/index.html

Just like the title says—this is the *Ally McBeal* quote page. And what does it feature? Quotes. Just quotes. Its devotion to a single topic is refreshing. There are no cast bios. No episode summaries. Not even a single picture. How admirable. If you've temporarily overdosed on shots of Calista Flockhart's winsome smile, this is the place to be. It's also the place to be if you enjoy reading *Ally* dialogue snippets treated as if they were the wit and wisdom of Walt Whitman.

Added bonus: A copy of a letter from Flockhart her very own self to the site keeper. It's actually a rejection letter—Flockhart declining the cyberfan's offer to build her a Web site—but here in Happy *Ally* Land, it's designated as a "cool" artifact.

17. The Ally McBeal *Filing Cabinet*

http://ovrdedge.simplenet.com/ally/entries1.html

Okay, so let's say you can't remember the name of the inflatable doll-man that popped up in the Season No. 1 episode entitled "Happy Birthday, Baby." Now, it's not like you need to know what the doll was called, but, well, you want to know. It's sort of like a test. (Did you imagine the doll

had a name?) It's also a matter of principle. Are *Star Trek* fans, you ask indignantly, the only fans allowed to be obsessive about their TV? Are they the only ones to wallow in minutiae, down to the alleged breakfast-eating habits of Klingons? Of course not. Feel free to surf on over to this *Ally* site—and wallow at will.

This is a good encyclopedic rundown of characters and character catchphrases, indexed by season, by episode and/or by alphabet. Oh, and the name of that inflatable boy-toy? David. Found it under *D*.

18. Ally McBeal *[Roger Wilco]*

http://wonko.inow.com/wilco/entertainment/allymcbeal/index.html

A general fan show site with the requisite episode guide, cast bios and roundup of so-called McBealisms. It's far from the most authoritative site available. (Looks like the episode guide pretty much petered out midway through the first season—last time we checked, anyway.) But it gets a nod here for its virtual *Ally* postcards. E-mail your friends a picture of Calista Flockhart. It's no Hallmark, but it'll do for *Ally* fans.

19. Dancing Baby Stuff

You could write a book much longer than we care to on the ins and outs of where to find that creepy computer tot on the Web. We'll save you some time (and some poor trees, in the process).

If you must visit two Dancing Baby sites, then go here: The Official Dancing Baby Page (http://ourworld.compuserve.com/homepages/rlussier/); and then go here: The Unofficial Dancing Baby Homepage (http://www.nwlink.com/~xott/ babypage.htm). The first site will tell you the story of how Baby Cha-Cha was born (by the guy, Ron Lussier, who birthed him); the second site will let you gawk at the number of Dancing Baby spawns on the Web (with link after link after link after . . .). If you must go to a third site, please first consult a trained psychiatric professional.

THE STAR STUFF

20. Just Calista Flockhart

http://www.geocities.com/Hollywood/Boulevard/9865/

Log on here for the chance to join the "cult" of Calista. As cults go, it seems pretty tame. No spiked Kool-Aid recipes being passed around here. No, the Calista "cult" is just a list of like-minded fans. You type in your name, e-mail, age and Web-site affiliation (if any)—then fraternize at your leisure. See? Pretty tame. About the scariest thing is the birthday thing. Take a look at the "cult" members' ages and you learn that most of the leading *Ally* pages, including this one, are designed and maintained by young-'uns, age eighteen and under. If you're older than eighteen, you may need a moment to fully comprehend just how quickly the world made you obsolete. When you recover, check out the site's ultra-earnest top-ten reasons why Ally McBeal is a lovable character—including something about how she wouldn't date a bald guy just to be politically correct.

21. The New Calista Flockhart Webpage

http://www4.ncsu.edu/~jcmcmurr/ally/

Your basic—albeit well-organized and attractive—shrine to the *Ally* star, with pictures, bio, a chat room and a discussion page. Distinguishing feature: the "Why I Like *Ally McBeal*" section. Gotta love a site that's not too shy to gush.

22. Courtney Thorne-Smith Unofficial Home Page

http://www.geocities.com/Hollywood/Hills/6813/cts/index.html

Rates a mention because it was launched by a fan who claims to have been bewitched by Ms. CT-S upon first sight of her in the long-forgotten 1980s sitcom *Day by Day. Quelle dédication!* In fact, you almost feel good that Courtney Thorne-Smith turned out so well—that her career continued to grow—for the sake of others who must have been smitten so early. Honestly, what if you got hooked on Linda Kelsey (another *Day by Day*

costar)? What do you do with that energy? Kelsey may be leading a slap-happy life right now, but you can't share it—she hasn't been back in primetime, lo, these many years. (Old reruns of *Lou Grant*, another Kelsey show, don't count.) Anyway . . . If you want to longingly gaze at auto-graphed photos of you-know-who, this is the source. There's not a ton o' *Ally* stuff here, but there is a fairly good overview of Thorne-Smith's over-all career. Plus, in case you're kicking yourself for missing the actress's guest-star shot on a January 1997 episode of *Spin City*, fret no more—there's plenty of shots here to help you relive that little bit of tube history.

23. The Peter MacNicol Home Page

http://www.west.net/~phantm/index.html

Despite its name (and the Peter MacNicolesque signature ghosted in the background), this is a fan—not an official—site. (No scandal here—it's properly identified as such on the front page.) Authorized or no, this site is mucho complete—down to the actor's audiobook narration credits. Everything you wanted to know, and stuff you probably didn't even know you wanted to know, about John Cage's doppelgänger is here for the read-ing. (The actor's reputed favorite color? Teal green. Who knew?) It gets points, too, for being launched in 1996—before the dawn of *Ally*. Also a good stop for fans of MacNicol's first David E. Kelley series, *Chicago Hope*.

24. The Unofficial Lisa Nicole Carson Webpage by Jessica

http://members.tripod.com/~asseJ/lisa.html

About time this *Ally* costar got her own fan site—and here it is. Now, it's not the most elaborate of cyber renderings and it's not hooked up to any Lisa Nicole Carson Webring (no such thing exists), but the site builder deserves kudos simply for refusing to contribute yet another *Ally* and/or Calista Flockhart tribute to the Web. Is Carson not on the series, too? If you snub her in cyberspace, does she not . . . um, bleed? Mixed-up metaphors aside, the point here is Carson deserves at least what this sin-cere site affords: pictures, a filmography, a listing of vital stats. When

you're done enjoying that stuff, check out the author's "Get to Know Sarah Jessica Parker" page. What's a Sarah Jessica Parker link doing here? No idea. Maybe it's a people-with-three-word-name thing. (Although, strangely, no Courtney Thorne-Smith link here.)

25. Gregg's Unofficial Vonda Shepard Page

http://www-scf.usc.edu/~gwagener/vonda.html

A solid companion/alternative to the Vesper Alley site, with brief audio snippets, a history of Shepard's album release dates, and a tracking report of upcoming tour and TV appearances. If you doubt the power of music, check out the section that posts reader stories about their first-person encounters with Vonda. The tales (mostly about how people ran into her before, during or after a live show) are heartfelt as they paint Shepard as a kind soul with powers just a notch below healing the lame. If you're a soft touch, keep a Kleenex handy.

26. Michael Easton: Actor, Author, Director, Poet

http://www.michaeleaston.com/

A fan site about the guy who played the guy with the big penis. Seriously, this is very, very complete with an extensive bio, career updates and article links. The authoritative Michael Easton repository on the Web. And why not? God bless America.

27. Simply Jesse!

http://members.xoom.com/jessemartin/jesse.html

Hey, if the Dancing Twins merit their own Web site, why not a guy who actually spoke on the series? Why not, indeed. Which brings us to this, the Jesse L. Martin fan site, dedicated to the guy who appeared (and uttered dialogue) as nice-guy Dr. Greg Butters for a three-episode *Ally* stint in Season No. 1. In addition to *Ally* stuff, there's also info here on Martin's other notable projects: Broadway's *Rent* and TV's *413 Hope St.*

The best thing about smaller, less-traveled sites like this, though, lies in the daffy details. Like the merry-go-round-style keyboard version of "Cover Me" (Martin's big number from *Rent*) that plays on endless loop. Or the section that allows you to go on a so-called "virtual date" with the actor (i.e., a series of brief dialogue clips arranged to approximate date talk.) Bottom line: Very endearing.

EXTRA

Not listed above (because it's not a site) is the *Ally* Internet newsgroup: alt.tv.ally-mcbeal. A prime meeting/sharing/dishing ground. The newsgroup is easily found through the Deja News site at: http://www.dejanews.com.

Appendix B
How to Contact Ally Stars

THE SERIES
Ally McBeal
c/o Manhattan Beach Studios
1600 Rosecrans Ave.
Building 4-A, 3rd Floor
Manhattan Beach, CA 90266

(The best, first stop for fan mail, photo requests. As is the custom, if you're asking for something back—like a photo—be sure to include a self-addressed, stamped envelope.)

THE STARS
(The following contact addresses for the *Ally* cast were accurate as of this book's publication.)

Calista Flockhart
c/o The Gersh Agency
P.O. Box 5617
Beverly Hills, CA 90210

Courtney Thorne-Smith
c/o Paradigm Talent
10100 Santa Monica Blvd., Suite 2500
Los Angeles, CA 90067

Greg Germann
c/o Writers & Artists
924 Westwood Blvd., Suite 900
Los Angeles, CA 90024

Lisa Nicole Carson
(No contact information available. Try the *Ally* studios.)

Jane Krakowski
c/o Sutton, Barth & Vennari
145 S. Fairfax Ave., Suite 310
Los Angeles, CA 90036

Peter MacNicol
c/o InHouse Entertainment
7720 Sunset Blvd.
Los Angeles, CA 90046

Gil Bellows
c/o William Morris
151 El Camino Drive
Beverly Hills, CA 90212

Vonda Shepard
c/o Vesper Alley Records
23852 Pacific Coast Highway, Suite 920
Malibu, CA 90265

The Dancing Twins (Steve and Eric Cohen)
e-mail: allytwin1@aol.com; allytwin2@aol.com

Bibliography

ARTICLES AND PRESS RELEASES

Adalian, Josef. "Bernhard Feels at Home in *Ally*'s Legal Pad." (Sandra Bernhard profile) *New York Post*, November 10, 1997.

—. "It's Holliday Time on Tonight's *McBeal*." (Jennifer Holliday profile) *New York Post*, December 1, 1997, p. 74.

Adams, Jane Meredith. "Calista Flockhart Finds Fame as Ally McBeal." *Biography*, February 1998, p. 82–85, 117.

"*Ally McBeal* Premiere Posts Fox's Highest Rating for Any Series Premiere in Time Period Since 1989," Fox press release, 1997.

"*Ally* Scene Gives Thorne-Smith Exposure." (Courtney Thorne-Smith's bare-bottom shot) *USA Today*, May 15, 1998.

Barney, Chuck. "Ally-oop: Calista Flockhart Basks in *McBeal* Appeal." Knight-Ridder News Service, December 1, 1997.

Bauder, David. "Five Questions for Vonda Shepard." Associated Press, July 8, 1998.

Bellafante, Ginia. "Feminism: It's All About Me!" (Social commentary) *Time*, June 29, 1998, p. 54–62.

Bianculli, David. "*Ally* Guest a Crossover Hit as Transsexual." (Review of Season No. 1 episode "Boy to the World.") *New York Daily News*, December 1, 1997.

—. "An Appealing *Ally McBeal*." (Review) *New York Daily News*, September 8, 1997.

—. "Right Up Her *Ally*." (Calista Flockhart profile) *New York Daily News' New York Vue*, January 4, 1998, p. 3.

Bickley, Claire. "Twins Double Their Pleasure." (Dancing Twins profile) *Toronto Sun*, November 17, 1997.

Blau, Eleanor. "Save the Penny—Her Thoughts Are Giveaways." *New York Times* (date unknown).

Brantley, Ben. "*Rent.*" (Stage review of musical, with Jesse L. Martin) *New York Times*, February 14, 1996.

—. "Surviving on Grace in a World Beyond Hope." (Stage review of *Three Sisters*, with Calista Flockhart) *New York Times*, February 14, 1997.

Braxton, Greg. "The Flaws Help." (Calista Flockhart profile) *Los Angeles Times' TV Times*, September 21–27, 1997, p. 16.

—. "How *Ally* Complicates Flockhart's Life." (Calista Flockhart profile) *Los Angeles Times*, September 9, 1998, p. F9.

Brown, Ann. "Hollywood's Gypsy Woman." (Lisa Nicole Carson profile) *Black Elegance*, September 1998, p. 46–51.

Carson, Tom. "Show Me the Bunny!" (Review) *Village Voice*, October 7, 1997.

Carter, Bill. "*Ally* Commercials." (Item about Season No. 1 episode "The Playing Field.") *New York Times*, March 18, 1998.

—. "The Unintended Career of TV's Prolific Writer." (David E. Kelley) *New York Times*, March 2, 1998, p. B1, 9.

Casablanca, Ted. "The Awful Truth: Skirting the Issue." (Calista Flockhart's skirt hems) E! Online (www.eonline.com), April 2, 1998.

Chambers, Veronica. "How Would Ally Do It?" *Newsweek*, March 2, 1998, p. 58–60.

Champagne, Christine. "Calista Flockhart: Being *Ally McBeal*." GIST TV (www.gisttv.com).

Collins, James. "Woman of the Year." (Poses the question: Is Ally McBeal "confused and lov-able" or a "simpering drag"?) *Time*, September 10, 1997.

"Daily Dish: *Ally* Oops! *McBeal* Vanishes After Big Win." (On series' production schedule) TVGen (www.tvgen.com), February 5, 1998.

"Dancing Baby Dabbling in Music." *Hollywood Reporter*, April 14, 1998.

"Dancing Baby Hits Stores Soon." CNET's News.com, published in *New York Post*, July 22, 1998.

"David E. Kelley Creates a Fox Signature Drama Sure to Be One of 1997's Most Talked About New Series," Fox press release, 1997.

DeRosa, Robin. "*Ally* Makes Appeal to Men." (Calista Flockhart profile) *USA Today*, October 20, 1997, p. D1.

DeVries, Hilary. "Ally Chat." (Q&A with Calista Flockhart, Lisa Nicole Carson, Jane Krakowski) *TV Guide*, September 26, 1998.

—. "Cannon's Law." (Dyan Cannon profile) *TV Guide*, February 22, 1998.

Elber, Lynn. "Five Questions: Calista Flockhart." Associated Press, January 2, 1998.

—. "Giggle TV: Girls Are In, Women Out." Associated Press, June 8, 1998.

—. "HBO's *Earth to Moon* Leads Emmy Nods." (1997–98 Primetime Emmy nominations) Associated Press, July 24, 1998.

Epstein, Jeffrey. "Ally McBeal's Sexy Assistant." (Jane Krakowski profile) *Soap Opera News*, May 12, 1998, p. 30–33.

Errico, Marcus and Daniel Frankel. "Golden Globes '98: The Winners Are …." (Calista Flockhart's reaction to award win) E! Online (www.eonline.com), January 5, 1998.

Fleming, Michael. "Dish: Celebs See Red After Mags Go to Bed." (David E. Kelley's dialogue gets back at *Entertainment Weekly*) *Daily Variety*, 1997.

"For Michael Easton, *Ally* Is a Steppingstone to Stardom." *USA Today*, August 14, 1998.

"Fox Picks Up New Hit *Ally McBeal* for Full Season," Fox press release, 1997.

Garron, Barry. "*Ally McBeal*." (Review of *Ally/Practice* crossover episodes) *Hollywood Reporter*, April 27, 1998, p. 9, 14.

Gates, Anita. "*Chairman of the Board:* An Inventor and Heir Nonapparent." (Film review of Carrot Top opus, costarring Courtney Thorne-Smith) *New York Times,* March 14, 1998.

"Gil Bellows: Georgia—and Ally—on his mind." *TV Guide,* February 14, 1998.

Glynn, Michael. "Ally McBeal Finally Finds Her Mr. Right!" (About Calista Flockhart's friend Cedric Harris) *National Enquirer,* January 24, 1998, p. 2.

—. "Real-Life Love Triangle for *Ally.*" (Calista Flockhart's rumored romance with producer Jeffrey Kramer) *National Enquirer,* June 9, 1998.

Goldsmith, Olivia. "Word-Perfect Women: Out of the Mouths of Babes." (Op-ed piece about series) *New York Times,* December 7, 1997.

Gorov, Lynda. "Where's Boston? OK, So Faneuil Hall Is in Pasadena, But *Ally McBeal* Still Captures the Reality of a Woman of the '90s." (About series' real/reel geography; Calista Flockhart profile) *Boston Globe,* October 20, 1997, p. C9.

Graff, Gary. "*Ally McBeal* singer wants to make her own name." (Vonda Shepard profile) Reuters News Agency, June 5, 1998.

Graham, Jefferson. "*Ally McBeal* creator Kelley surprised with her success." *USA Today,* January 12, 1998, p. D3.

—. "*Ally, Practice* are movin' on up." (About crossover episodes) *USA Today,* July 15, 1998.

—. "For Thorne-Smith, everything's coming up Mel-roses." *USA Today,* February 16, 1994, p. D3.

—. "In Tune with *Ally.*" (Vonda Shepard profile) *USA Today,* May 4, 1998.

—. "Kelley Makes Case for Courtroom Crossover." *USA Today,* April 27, 1998, p. D3.

—. "Peter MacNicol, Bellying Up to the Bar." *USA Today,* December 15, 1997, p. D3.

Greene, Robin L. "New Local Couple Has Hollywood Ties." (Profile of Calista Flockhart's parents) *Morristown* (TN) *Tribune,* November 11, 1997, p. A1, 7.

Grice, Elizabeth. "A Full Life: Still 'Cary Grant's Ex-wife to Some, Dyan Cannon Enjoys Life on Her Own." *Chicago Sun-Times,* December 31, 1997.

Hall, Carla. "Crosstown Crossover." (Review of *Ally/Practice* crossover episodes) *TV Guide,* April 5, 1998, p. 7.

Heffley, Lynne. "*Lifestories:* Gritty Survival Tips for Families." (Review of *The Secret Life of Mary-Margaret: Portrait of a Bulimic,* with Calista Flockhart) *Los Angeles Times,* October 13, 1992, p. F11.

Helligar, Jeremy and Lisa Kay Greissinger. "Dream Team." (About Nick and Nora pajamas) *People,* May 18, 1998, p. 109–10.

Hochman, Steve. "Sony to Float *Ally McBeal* Soundtrack." *Los Angeles Times,* March 27, 1998, p. F8.

Hontz, Jenny. "Fox Orders More *McBeal.*" *Daily Variety,* October 9, 1997, p. 1.

Huff, Richard. "*Ally's* Fish Turns into Big Catch." (Greg Germann profile) *New York Daily News,* May 4, 1998.

Jacobs, Khalil. "Lisa Nicole Carson: Prime Time's Sexiest Woman." *Black Men,* July 1998, p. 39–40.

James, Caryn. "A Young Lawyer and Her Fantasies." (Review) *New York Times,* September 8, 1997.

"Japanese Men Like Janet Reno." Reuters News Service, November 21, 1997.

Jarvis, Jeff. "The Couch Critic: *Ally McBeal*." (Review) *TV Guide*, September 20–26, 1997.

Jefferson, Margo. "You Want to Slap Ally McBeal, but Do You Like Her?" *New York Times*, March 18, 1998.

Johnson, Ted. "Character Witness." (Peter MacNicol profile) *TV Guide*, June 13, 1998, p. 38–42.

—. "It's My Potty." (About *Ally*'s unisex set) *TV Guide*, February 28, 1998, p. 22.

—. "Lawyers in Love." (Series profile) *TV Guide*, February 28, 1998, p. 16–22.

Jordan, Julie. "Bytes: Baby Boom." (Dancing Baby profile) *People*, 1998.

Kellcher, Terry. "Tube: *Ally McBeal*." (Review) *People*, September 1997.

"Kelley, David. E." *Current Biography*, May 1998, p. 40–42.

Kitman, Marvin. "Getting to Know McBeal." (David E. Kelley's pre-*Ally* series ideas for Fox) *Newsday*, February 9, 1998.

Kuczynski, Alex. "Calista Comes Clean." *Bazaar*, September 1998, p. 502–505, 550–552.

Kloer, Phil. "Actress Takes on Tall Order as New *Ally* Cast Member." (Portia de Rossi profile) Cox News Service, September 14, 1998.

Lanthrop, Jason. "Joe, Jane Join in John." (About real-world unisex bathrooms) ABC-NEWS.com, June 11, 1998.

Lennon, Rosemarie. "Why Ally McBeal Beauty Was Told: YOU CAN'T ACT." *Star*, March 3, 1998, p. 17.

Levin, Gary. "Clothes Merchandisers Consider Trying Ally McBeal on for Size." *Newsday*, June 12, 1998, p. E1.

Lipton, Michael A. with Cynthia Wang. "Taking a Bough." (Jane Krakowski profile) *People*, July 20, 1998, p. 87–88.

Lipton, Michael A. with Lyndon Stambler. "TV's Tin Pan *Ally* Strikes Gold." (Vonda Shepard profile) *People*, June 1, 1998.

Logan, Michael. "Jane's World." (Jane Krakowski profile) *TV Guide*, August 22, 1998.

Lussier, Ron. "The REAL Baby Story." The Official Dancing Baby [Web] Page (ourworld.compuserve.com/homepages/rlussier/).

Marder, Keith. "Laying Down Kelley's Law." (David E. Kelley profile) *Los Angeles Daily News*, April 26, 1998, L.A. Life section, p. 3, 6.

Martinez, Julio. "*413 Hope St.* Premiere Formulaic." (Review) *Daily Variety*, September 15, 1997.

Mink, Eric. "*Ally*: Soph Far, Soph Great." (Review of Season No. 2 opener, "The Real World.") *New York Daily News*, September 14, 1998.

—. "When *Larry* Met *Ally*… " (About the Garry Shandling–Calista Flockhart "summit") *New York Daily News*, July 21, 1998, p. 70.

Modderno, Craig. "*Ally McBeal*'s Songstress Gets the Last Laugh." (Vonda Shepard profile) TVGen (www.tvgen.com), February 9, 1998.

Moore, Scott. "The Heartfelt Soul of *Ally McBeal*." (Vonda Shepard profile) *Washington Post*, April 25, 1998.

Morice, Laura. "Bringing Ally to Life." (Calista Flockhart profile) *Self*, February 1998, p. 24.

"My Favorite Weekend: Greg Germann." *Los Angeles Times*, January 22, 1998, p. F7.

"Newsmakers: Boogie Baby on Board." (Dancing Baby profile) *Newsweek,* August 3, 1998.

Pergament, Alan. "Attractive *Ally McBeal* Co-Star Talks of Insecurity and Men." (Courtney Thorne-Smith profile) *Buffalo News,* April 15, 1998.

"Peter MacNicol Joins *Ally McBeal* as a Series Regular; Jennifer Holliday and Wilson Cruz Guest Star Dec. 1," Fox press release, 1997.

Pope, Clementina. "Jersey Girl Makes California Hotter." (Interview with Jane Krakowski's mother) William Patterson University's *Cybernews,* September 28, 1998.

"Portia de Rossi Joining *Ally McBeal,*" Bragman, Nyman, Cafarelli press release, 1998.

Rafferty, Terrence. "That Girl: With a good job, plenty of feelings and great outfits, yuppie TV's Ally McBeal wants to be the thinking man's sex kitten—if she only had a brain." *GQ,* February 1998, p. 61, 64.

"Return Engagements: Courtney Thorne-Smith." *People,* October 5, 1998, p. 65.

"Returning Favorites: *Ally McBeal.*" *TV Guide,* September 2, 1998.

Rice, Lynette and Jonathan Davies. "Fox Affils Angry Over *Ally* Stunt." (*Ally/Practice* crossover episodes) *Hollywood Reporter,* March 20, 1998, p. 1, 64.

Richardson, David. "*Ally McBeal:* Daydream Believer." *TV Zone,* Issue #104, p. 32–36.

Rochlin, Margy. "The *Us* Interview: Calista Flockhart." *Us,* May 1998, p. 55–58.

Rosenberg, Howard. "*Ally McBeal* Is Carefree—and Flimsy." (Review) *Los Angeles Times,* September 8, 1997, p. F8.

—. "Disorder in Court When *Practice, Ally* Mix." (Review of *Ally/Practice* crossover episodes) *Los Angeles Times,* April 27, 1998, p. F1, 14.

Roush, Matt. "Totally Original *Ally.*" (Review of Season No. 1 Episode "One Hundred Tears Away") *USA Today,* October 20, 1997, p. D3.

Royce, Brenda Scott. "An Interview with … Greg Germann." *Viewers Voice,* February 1998.

Rush, George and Joanna Molloy. "Rush & Molloy: Insider—*Ally* star is an attorney-at-love." (Calista Flockhart reps deny Jeffrey Kramer romance) *New York Daily News,* May 14, 1998, p. 14.

Ryan, James. "Like Her Character, *Melrose Place* Star Puts Premium on Friends." (Courtney Thorne-Smith profile) BPI Entertainment News Wire, November 1992.

Schaefer, Stephen. "Good neighbor at *Melrose Place.*" (Courtney Thorne-Smith profile) *USA Today,* September 10, 1992, p. D8.

Scheerer, Mark. "Shepard Success Reaches from Overnight to Prime Time." *CNN Interactive,* May 26, 1998.

Schneider, Karen S. "Arguing Her Case." (Calista Flockhart answers anorexia rumors) *People,* November 9, 1998, p. 92–101.

Schwed, Mark. "Hollywood Grapevine." (Portia de Rossi's early law ambitions) *TV Guide,* August 14, 1998.

Scott, Vernon. "Oh, What Is So Rare … " (Michael Easton profile) *Hollywood Reporter,* September 18, 1997.

Scott, Walter. "Personality Parade." (Factoid about David E. Kelley's grandmother, Mildred) *Parade,* May 10, 1998, p. 2.

Starr, Michael. "Golden Girl Ally's Real Appeal." (Calista Flockhart profile) *New York Post,* January 20, 1998, p. 82.

Steinhauer, Jennifer. "How to Succeed in Business Without Really Trying on a Suit." (TV fashion) *New York Times,* September 27, 1997.

Svetkey, Benjamin. "Everything You Love or Hate About *Ally McBeal.*" *Entertainment Weekly,* January 30, 1998, p. 22–26.

—. "Kelley's Heroes." (Calista Flockhart/Dylan McDermott cover story) *Entertainment Weekly,* September 25, 1998, p. 33–40.

Vigoda, Arlene. "Ally's Hemlines Really Inching Up." *USA Today,* October 12, 1998, p. 3D.

Waggoner, Martha. "*Ally* Fans Choose Theme Songs." (Season No. 1 Episode "Theme of Life") Associated Press, May 11, 1998.

Wallenfels, Jessica. "*Ally McBeal*'s Mass Appeal." (*Ally* tribute at Museum of Television and Radio's William S. Paley Television Festival) Ultimate TV (www.ultimatetv.com), March 27, 1998.

Weeks, Janet. "The players in *Ally*'s court." *USA Today,* February 23, 1998, p. D3.

Weinstein, Steve. "Can *Ally* Bring New Business to *Practice?*" *Los Angeles Times,* April 25, 1998, p. F1, 17.

Werts, Diane. "A Pro TV—Viewer's Picks." (Review) *Newsday,* October 28, 1997.

"Why Michelle Pfeiffer Is Real-Life Ally McBeal." *Star,* February 24, 1998, p. 35.

Willman, Chris. "Kelley's Hero Vonda Shepard Plays It Cool." *Entertainment Weekly,* January 30, 1998, p.24–25.

Wloszdzyna, Susan. "Net's Dancing Baby Goes Prime Time." *USA Today,* January 1, 1998.

Zaslow, Jeffrey. "Straight Talk … with Lisa Nicole Carson." *USA Weekend,* May 17, 1998.

Zurawik, David. "Stepping Backward with Ally." *Baltimore Sun,* March 1, 1998.

BOOKS

Farnighetti, Robert. *The World Almanac and Book of Facts.* New Jersey: Funk & Wangalls Corp., 1994.

Maltin, Leonard (editor). *Leonard Maltin's 1997 Movie & Video Guide.* New York: Penguin Books, 1996.

McNeil, Alex. *Total Television.* New York: Penguin Books, 1996.

WEB SITES

In addition to the *Ally* sites listed in Appendix A, the following Web sites were consulted in preparation of this book: Ally McBeal newsgroup (alt.tv.ally-mcbeal), Amazon.com (www.amazon.com), Billboard Online (www.billboard.com), CD Now (www.cdnow.com), Celebsite (www.celebsite.com), E! Online (www.eonline.com), ET Online (www.etonline.com), Fox (www.fox.com), Internet Movie Database (www.imdb.com), Mr. Showbiz! (www.mrshowbiz.com) and NBC (www.nbc.com).

INTERVIEWS, ONLINE CHATS AND OTHER SOURCES

America Online, chat with Vonda Shepard, December 15, 1997.

E! Online (www.eonline.com), "The Star Boards … with Greg Germann."

E! Online (www.eonline.com), "Q&A … with Tracey Ullman."

ET Online (www.etonline.com), Q&A with Calista Flockhart, June 1998.

ET Online (www.etonline.com), Q&A with Courtney Thorne-Smith, June 1998.

Entertainment Tonight interview with Michael Easton, broadcast July 13, 1998.

Fox Entertainment Group 1998 Media Briefing by Peter Roth, May 21, 1998.

Late Night with Conan O'Brien, interview with Courtney Thorne-Smith, broadcast May 22, 1998.

Nielsen Television Ranking Report, 1997–98 season.

Talk City (www.talkcity.com), chat with Peter MacNicol, May 18, 1998.

U.S. Government Official bio of Attorney General Janet Reno (www.usdoj.gov/bios/jreno.html).

Ultimate TV chat with Eric & Steve Cohen (aka the Dancing Twins)

Viewers for Quality Television Conference on Quality Television (transcript), September 26, 1997.

Viewers for Quality Television Conference on New Series (video record), September 27, 1997.

Index